THE SACRED SPIRAL

UNLOCKING THE INDIVIDUAL'S INFINITE POTENTIALS

DRACAENA A. PAXX

THE SACRED SPIRAL:
Unlocking The Individual's Infinite Potentials
Copyright © 2024 by Dracaena A. Paxx

ISBN: 979-8895310588 (sc)

ISBN: 979-8895310595 (e)

All rights reserved. No part of this publication may be reproduced, distributed, or transmitted in any form or by any means, including photocopying, recording, or other electronic or mechanical methods, without the prior written permission of the publisher and/or the author, except in the case of brief quotations embodied in critical reviews and other noncommercial uses permitted by copyright law.

The views expressed in this book are solely those of the author and do not necessarily reflect the views of the publisher, and the publisher hereby disclaims any responsibility for them.

Writers' Branding
(877) 608-6550
www.writersbranding.com
media@writersbranding.com

CONTENTS

DEDICATION v
INTRODUCTION vii

THE SACRED SPIRAL 1
    THE BEGINNING 3
    DRACONIC BASICS EXPLAINED 5
    THE BRUCE AND THE SPIDER, A SCOTTISH LEGEND 11

HAVE CONFIDENCE- YOU ARE BETTER THAN YOU THINK! 13
    FAERY MAID OF ASTOLAT 29

DRACONIC PHILOSOPHIES AND UNDERSTANDINGS 41
    STRENGTH 43

CONTINUING OUR JOURNEY 67
    THE RITUAL ITSELF EXPLANATIONS 69
    YEARLY SABBATS 81
    MEDICRIN 107
    YEARLY PERSONAL RITUALS 109
    APPOINTMENT IN SAMARRA 117
    HANDFASTINGS 143
    INCENSES AND USES 159
    CITATIONS 163

DEDICATION

This book is dedicated to the knowledgeable, thoughtful, and awesome Joseph Campbell. I highly recommend his books, videos, and audio. He brought and explained Mythology in a human philosophy to be utilized by all people. H strongly inspired my work as I wish to go a step further and Intend to bring the philosophies and spirituality to each person's life, defining how to be spiritual on a day-to-day basis. A person does not need to spend One day per week pursuing a spiritual life. This can be done daily through basic practices and philosophies explained in THE SACRED SPIRAL - a book by DRACAENA PAXX.

    This book is dedicated to Joseph Campbell. He was a great teacher to all. He devoted his life to the study of comparative mythology worldwide. He helped interpret the meaning of mythology, the psychology behind the stories and legends of mythology, and psychology to humanity for use in our daily lives. In everyday life, he made this understanding possible for all. In the SACRED SPIRAL, I intend to follow his excellent example and go one step further. I wish to help illustrate how to bring spiritual acts into daily life. A particular building or a once-a-week meditation is not enough; many know this and seek answers. My goal is to help many people find those answers. It does not matter the faith of any person. We all speak the same language, using different words. Faith is the most important. The oldest form of the Old Testament states Keep Holy the Sabbath and **Remember the teachings of the Sabbath!** These I intend to illustrate in **THE SACRED SPIRAL.**

INTRODUCTION

The purpose of this book is that I wish it to validate and empower all genuine spiritual seekers. I pass this wisdom I have acquired through physical teachers and the universal energies. My physical teacher passed on, and there was no one to work with but myself and my family that I know of to pass this to. He always told me that spirituality had its basis in science, for physical and spiritual thought were parts of the balance. After his passing, I spent time understanding this through Quantum Physics.

The discussion is tailored to the audience at hand. So many people get scared because they do not understand Physics. They lump it into the hard-to-understand. If Quantum Physics were communicated correctly about the beauty and necessity of understanding this subject, I would hope more people would change their viewpoints about science. This, I feel, makes a beautiful vehicle for such a thing. Quantum Physics embraces the nonlinear sciences and creative and imaginative thought.

By definition, Quantum physics studies the minor parts of life. Atoms, matter, energy, vibrations, and study of the natural world and its phenomena. Galileo and Newton were coined as heretics, stating that the scientific and religious worlds worked in unison. They both explained the other, just in different words. The Theory of Everything loosely describes vibrations and dimensions. Magnetism is self-explanatory as karma.

Paradoxes abound- as in many of the deities in this book. These are embodiments of opposites that allow growth and unity. The science of Quantum Physics invites us to study the universe and how it affects us. Spiritually and physically. It is a long-held belief that one explains the other. Draconis embraces these practices.

This subject I use to help people open their minds and not be afraid to think and be daring in their thoughts. If more people tried to understand, the world would not have the problems they do now. Yes, they would be there but more challenging, and people would try to solve them, not be afraid to use their minds. Many people fear big words, so I broke them down to make them easier to understand. If a person understands what a thing is about, they are not afraid to discover it!

I learned to understand much more. For example, theorists wish to prove their hypotheses or thoughts. We may be correct, but we must test our theories to find out! Another example is Karma and the Law of Magnetism!!

I know that the Universal Energies are all different, and many interpret them differently, yet when many people have the same thought and results- it is true!!

THE SACRED SPIRAL

THE BEGINNING

Many years ago, a girl spent time alone in a remote land. She was very young, about five or six years of age. She was prone to many different hallucinations- or so many thought and told her repeatedly, saying: "ITS JUST YOUR IMAGINATION PLAYING TRICKS ON YOU; NOTHING HAS HAPPENED." Then, one night, she was woken by a disturbing deep, almost monstrous call. "ALICE, ALICE!" The deep monstrous voice kept calling. "COME WITH ME!" She roused and sat in bed, trying to figure out what this was. Then, floating directly in front of her was a sight that terrified her!

A giant black monster was in front of her. It had a long snout and wings with gold eyes. It kept calling to her, "ALICE, COME JOIN ME NOW," the girl, Alice, kept calling for help. No one seemed to hear her. "ALICE, COME WITH ME NOW," it kept repeating as she called for help. Finally, after a time, what seemed like hours, the being disappeared, and Alice ran to the safety of her parent's bed. The following day she rose and knew not to tell anyone what happened. They would only dismiss her, calling it another hallucination. She had what is termed Epilepsy and had been given antiepileptic and mind-altering drugs.

Years later, as she began her Draconic studies with us, she recounted the story again, for the discussion was about meeting one's Soul Dragon. She told of how she had been followed and received many teachings from an enormous Black dragon with gold eyes. His energy was so dense it was paradoxical, happy, and terrifying all at the same. She learned that many have strange experiences and supposed hallucinations to explain this away by many "Normal" people. But, the Elders told her her Soul Dragon had approached her. Looking back at her memories, she realized this was what had happened. Through the years, Alice learned from many Mystics, Teachers, and Scientists that those with Neurological disabilities, like epilepsy, can see and experience other realms and feel energy shifts in different dimensions...

DRACONIC BASICS EXPLAINED

FREEDOM OF PERSONALIZATION AND INTUITION

I have faith in humans as a whole! You are all stronger and much more intelligent than yourself credit for. Because of this, I will not talk down to you. Instead, I trust you to follow your intuition.

If you feel something you wish to research further, I trust you to do it. I will give you the basics of living life with spirituality, or even the philosophies and understanding added into your daily life.

MANY LEARNING STYLES

The Circle of Bards

One of the ways a Celt prefers to learn. Each Bardic group will have its Ollamh (Teacher), Helping many Folchlachs (Beginners). Many will share knowledge and ideas.

Think back to your favorite teacher! They were so probably because they made you feel good about yourself, which is our goal.

People will not hear the Creative Muse unless they feel good about themselves. There will be many exercises within each group to help each person to get better at what they wish to accomplish

Exercises are done with constructive criticism, helpful suggestions, and praise and comments from others. Kind words are a must here, for if one feels not validated in their craft but ashamed, they will never pursue this again!

The exercises all Ollamhs/teachers of each group know will be shared with all in the Circle as they progress. Many of these people will inspire others to create and share their progression with those in the group.

The guides keep the exercises repetitive and short, helping people and empowering others.

The differing creative muses do strike us at differing times. However, we do wish to create with other groups and grow.

A BIT ABOUT DRACONIS

I have spent many years seeking an honorable tradition and found the Celtic variation of the Germanic- Norse Draconic path most suited to my philosophy and psychology.

I found it very important to detail the workings of the Draconic Tradition for many years. For the most part, many people are very linear and seem to have difficulty understanding Draconis's abstractness and tolerance of Tradition.

Old-world practitioners use these theories as a basis for much mystical understanding, for it was from an old-world German Priest/Master that this was passed on to me. Unfortunately, my teacher Prideth passed on. He came to America from Bitburg, Germany, and I don't know of other practitioners in America. I never asked. He passed away several years after we connected. I speak to him in the 'other' "Dimension" and have gained much wisdom from him and many others.

Draconis is very ancient and goes back to Germany's Celtic-Nordic division. Before the division of the Celtic and Roman lands. When the division of the Rhine was occurring, many people said this was much like the Anglo-Saxon tradition, or Asatru, with certain aspects of shamanism, of course!!! I will not claim this to be different, yet many detailed, delicate parts of this tradition are. I am a spiritual purist and teach that way. All blood is true blood- diabetic blood testers are great for this!!! Spirit flame is true alcohol-not the chemical YUK!!! But Everclear- Bacardi 151, sex magic is private. Be as accurate to the tradition/directions as possible. This, too, is a shamanic tradition; all traditions have many similarities.

As this is an ancient tradition, all authentic traditions will have similarities despite their history. That is the way of human psychology throughout the world. Therefore, I will not detail the genealogy of Draconis here. Instead, I follow a Celtic version as I radiate to that, and the energies I speak of here have Celtic origin Anyone who is curious and wishes to learn more can contact me!

DRACONIS TRADITION

The Draconis Tradition is a very ancient tradition going back to Nordic theology's height when the Nordic(1) gods and Goddesses known as the Asa(2) Gods abounded. Draconis is based on the workings of the Universal Dragon. I utilize many, Celtic tones and mundane words—Many who do not understand call this "Chaos Magic" (3). There are three types of Draconis.

One subdivision of Draconis is Asa Draconis. It is primarily patriarchal and martial. It has rules that must be followed, final, decisive, or judgmental. It is predominantly intolerant and closed. Asa, Draconis-named for the Asa Gods, is very solar-oriented and not for the faint of heart or dabblers. Nevertheless, this is an area of Draconis. One must understand before progressing unless they are happy to practice and grow.

Another subdivision of Draconis is Vana Draconis, named for the Vanir. It is feminine and life-oriented, utilizing light and dark's creative aspects. It helps one understand the beauty and horrors of both. Vanir Draconis is very lunar and ritualistic, waxing, full, and waning moons. It is very feminine and "Goddess oriented" Vana Draconis is not specific or 'writ in stone' as the process works with the 'Dragons, Faery, Divine, Universal, Deities OR any energies. There are laws to guide one, but they are very few. The threefold law is essential to learning and learning to "use" the laws we follow.

The third subdivision within Draconis is the Wyrd Draconis, Named for the Norns, Sisters of Wyrd. It instills many of the beliefs and practices of Asa and Vana. In Asa, one learns to follow every strict rule. In Vana, people know to be creative in their rituals and magic.

In Wyrd Draconis, one will work closely with many Deities in their aspects, working with light and dark forces. There will be a continual discussion with the practitioner and Deities, much in a nontraditional way. This is the area of Draconis where one learns to be Chaotic and Orderly, where one learns "Why " to break the rules. Plus, when breaking the rules CAN be done. Paradox's many purposes, destructive, terrible creations, and understanding of their existence. The members are of different levels and ages, for Draconis harbors no grudges concerning the time or length of study, for it is neverending.

Wisdom is looked for, not necessarily a lengthy history of study. Perfect love and Perfect trust, Honor of all beings, and respect for life are demanded by this tradition, as one has perfect love for the Deities, such that it will flow over to all. Draconis works with the phases of the moon as "The Gathering of the Sphere" is extremely lunar oriented-the Sacred Circle that is practiced "Sphere" acknowledges all and uses Waxing, Full, and Dark Moon ceremonies (4). The Circle is cast according to the moon and its tides, as all elemental colors shift with these same tides. That is a portion of "Sphere Gatherings" and the Seasonal Solar and Lunar Sabbats.

NORDIC- Pertaining to the Germanic peoples of northern Europe. Esp. the Scandinavian ASA-things pertaining to the Gods of Asgard.

CHAOS MAGIC -Learned and used by the Draconic practitioners who know that Chaos and order work hand in hand. These forces are worked with after much study and understanding.

WAXING, FULL, AND DARK MOON CEREMONIES- these tides are worked with for the changes in the energy produced in Draconic magic.

DRACONIC SPHERE, BASICS

Wyrd Draconis is a Mystical lunar tradition utilizing a few Solar rites. Hence Samhain is the beginning of the dark lunar year as Beltane is the beginning of the light lunar year. The Quarter colors used also represent the Dragon's transformations through time. This book also has many rites in it to be inserted in the spell-working portion of the ritual.

Sabbats are always open. Working circles are reserved only for Draconic dedicates, initiates, or trusted visitors to work with you.

Differing rituals are used weekly or working circles-spheres. Charges of the Energies are done/ sacred words to be said. Dark and light moon, Spheres are always mainly spell-working only, and the moon energies are used in their corresponding directions.

DRACONIC ENERGY AND LEY LINES

Draconic energy is primarily concentrated in beings of Fey, Dragons, Angelic, and Otherworldly beings of light and dark energy. These beings that we see are known to be human interpretations of energy. They know this is what many humans understand. Therefore, all are of benefit to us. However, care must be taken when working with these beings, for their rules are not the same as ours; they may be chaotic and paradoxical.

When working with these, one must be knowledgeable and intuitive. Draconic and Fey energy is easily worked with through our world, such as energies of plant and animal life, stones, etc. Each plant/animal/stone has differing energy. If one meditates with it long enough, mingling their energy with the item and building a rapport with it, it will gradually take you to other realms through its hidden doorways.

Placing stones between you and the plant helps strengthen the bond, mainly if it is a specific stone to match the plant's energy and Deity. For beginners, it is suitable to start off large with an Oak, which has immense energy, than experience the detailed/smaller ones. All sacred/life energy attracts the Fey Draconic Beings, including rituals and sacred power circles. Animals as well are vessels of energy, and they all differ. All energy entering has doors within any elemental life, flames, smoke, water, earth, dust, or ashes.

Another aspect of Fey or Draconic energy is that it is interchangeable. The Draconic Beings will do so much easier because their many planes work on the same level of learning for one. Draconic energy utilizes what is known as Ley lines, and these are concentrations, Draconic, or energy lines either naturally or humanly created, sometimes ending in a vortex.

Ley Lines are magically charged power energy lines that run through, or over, the earth—much more concentrated "power spots" than just the raw normal earth's energy field many work with. These Ley lines can be worked with directly by a Draconic mage. Other terms for these can be Dragon breath, Dragon fire, and Dragons Blood- not incense☺. These are natural reservoirs of power and can be tapped into by any person who understands energy.

These can be doorways from other dimensions, which is not always good. These can be altered, but it is challenging because other beings need a lot of help. However, a Draconic mage who understands Chaos and Order energy MAY be able to work with these. An added benefit to this power, once a Mage learns to tap into it and knows the feel of authentic Draconic energy, is the immense power that can be called upon to augment or aid an energy field as in rituals and spell work.

THE BRUCE AND THE SPIDER, A SCOTTISH LEGEND

There was once a king of Scotland whose name was Robert Bruce. He needed to be brave and wise, for the times he lived were wild and rude. The King of England was at war with him, and had led a great army into Scotland to drive him out of the land.

Battle after battle had been fought. Six times had Bruce led his brave little army against his foes, and six times had his men been beaten and driven into flight. Then, at last, his army was scattered. He was forced to hide in the woods and lonely places.

One rainy day, Bruce lay on the ground under a crude shed, listening to the patter of the drops on the roof above him. He was tired and sick and ready to give up all hope. It seemed that there was no use for him to do anything more.

He saw a spider over his head, ready to weave her web. He watched her as she toiled slowly and with great care. She tried to throw her frail thread six times, falling short from one beam to another.

"Poor thing!" said Bruce: "You know what it is to fail."

But the spider did not lose hope with the sixth failure. With still more care, she made ready to try for the seventh time. Bruce almost forgot his troubles as he watched her swing herself on the slender line. Would she fail again? No! The thread was carried safely to the beam and fastened there.

"I will try a seventh time!" cried Bruce.

He arose and called his men together. He told them of his plans and sent them out with messages of cheer to his disheartened people. Soon there was an army of brave Scots-men around him. Another battle was fought, and the King of England returned to his own country.

I have heard it said that, after that day, no one by the name of Bruce would ever hurt a spider. The lesson that the little creature had taught the King was never forgotten.

HAVE CONFIDENCE- YOU ARE BETTER THAN YOU THINK!

LAWS AND ORDAINS

For the most part, Groups have specific rules within the law of the land. That land is California, within the United States of America. The Bill of Rights in the Constitution is where the many laws that upheld human rights would be found. However, now many of the old rules are very unreasonable. A person may follow them if they wish, but it is dishonorable to force them on another!

Many old laws/or words were created to protect the practitioner against persecution. Examples may be Besom- broom, Athame- knife, & Name- secret name.

After much time and reasoning together and reasoning with the Group, the elders form their specific "Laws."

Many old laws are kept for historical purposes and sentimentality's sake. Yet they do not change and grow as people change and grow.

A wise person knows when to use rules. Also, how not to bend them freely without thought of others or anyone but use the rules to do your work! People's age or ranking does not matter; they may not change any law for their selfish benefit. The change must be rational, within the law of the land, and for all.

Those who do not follow ethical rules put themselves in grave danger of all Seen and Unseen spirits' massive backlash.

The great wise people who create rules within each coven realize they make mistakes and leave room to change or improve them.

As such, no man-made law is writ firmly in stone.

HUMAN MAGICAL RIGHTS

All must first realize – that there is no one right way to do things! No one gets to tell you what is wrong unless the action is hurtful. There are as many ways as there are people! What may be a waste of time for one may be a lesson for another!

Listen and choose your words wisely, and use suggestions of your knowledge and experience, not unreasonable rules. To place a stringent regulation on another without good reason is disrespectful to not only yourself, but the other person, and the Deity! No one person is God-dess and decides when one must complete their magical training! Even Deity will not place these stringent rules upon a being.

However, if a person witnesses another overstepping their boundaries.

They can let the person know the action is not beneficial and why. Every person learns differently and in a different way! Remember that a person does not make Divine rules. One only knows how to understand and interpret them in their way! Hence "An it harm none do what ye will, to thine own self be true!

PRIDE AND SELF-CONFIDENCE VS. ARROGANCE

Many people believe that arrogance and Pride or Self Confidence are much the same! That is a common mistake, yet understand why it is made. Many honorable individuals believe that 'To be a truly honorable being,' one must not, or does not brag about themselves or make themselves out to be the "HERO" at the expense of others especially!

These Dishonorable acts may be intentional, with the person not knowing how hurtful they are. However, with an honorable person-teacher teaching true self-confidence, the actions will not be cruel noble intentions come. This is where temperance and balance are explained and understood. Ethical people must honestly watch themselves and their activities, continually asking what others may see. A person with an essential role in life must constantly do self-checkups. That is imperative!!

First, let me discuss or give some examples of dishonorable acts. Bragging about oneself for being self-important, belittling others, or trying to make others think better of you is never good. It is often construed as lying/bragging.

Mental games are never good to use on another person, primarily if you use their plight for your gain.

Now look at the prideful acts and ask yourself before placing judgment... Ask yourself, Is the person a caring person who will help those in need?

Charisma, love & confidence are magnetic. Therefore, people flock to the person of Honor who wishes to attract these "young-minded" persons and give them a knowledgeable view of things they can use to enhance their lives!

However, understand some pretend to be charismatic, loving, and happy! They put on a perfect act that others may quickly fall for. They know the tricks and will use you and your abilities. These people are what we may call FAKE!

A moral attitude and positive outlook on the "future" will radiate and may be confused as arrogance or wrongful pride. So please take a second look at the action before judging. These people help others and have magnetic personalities. But unfortunately, a genuinely magnetic personality is not always "Freely given." Sometimes we have to work for it.

To lead many in an honorable fashion, we must be like the "Pied Piper," leading *"by example"* and making others genuinely want to be around us. Of course, many people will come if we radiate love and caring with our charisma. But, on the other hand, if people fear approaching us, passion and caring help break the barrier!

MOTIVATED SELF-INTEREST AND HONOR

Many people seem to be confused by "waste of energy."

I will use many personal experiences to make my point, which is extremely important.

We have all come across people or experiences that much wrong us, take advantage of, and trample us.

So many people WILL not fight back or even argue for their Human Rights. WHY??

For instance, if a person has been "kicked" around and personally and wronged by many, they leave that situation to what they think is better. To their dismay, the fact they do not take any action creates a very chaotic situation.

These people do nothing and do not take any action to make a statement or stand up for their rights!! Instead, they use the excuse of Karma- which does not always work to help people right wrongs.

By not acting on their situation proactively, they state to the universe that it is all right for them to be taken advantage of. These things to happen to them, and for others to treat them wrongly! Sadly enough, the Deities will have minimal sympathy, for a person must stand up for themselves.

The Deities will help but only if it is asked and deserved.

I was told by these people, "We will go with the flow and wait it out," why waste the energy fighting?"

Ok, first, it is not a waste of energy to argue-" The massive amounts of wrong we have endured are no longer alright with us!" Yes, continually arguing with a stubborn person may be pointless. But let them be wrong! Leave the situation to honor yourself!

We are showing others we will always have honor and fight for ourselves and our people!!! That is never a waste of energy!!!!!!

That is personally **motivated self-interest**. Just think of who all are witnessing your actions!!

A person has the right to destroy what is theirs, their work, and start over. Karma has nothing to do with it!

INCENSES AND THEIR MANY USES

There are many types of Incense to use for many purposes. A very popular is smudging- It is a practice that clears negative energy by utilizing many herbs. Cedar, and Sage, are the most prominent for smudging. Smudging, if it is needed, is very simple. Take the herb, and burn it to release the smoke. Snudging, in some form, SHOULD help the energy leave or dissipate. An oil diffuser is just as effective with particular oils. Additionally, plant incenses/ energies are beneficial for Earthly powers as they are Earthly.

There are many reasons a thing is as it is. Many teachers understand and work magic and may have specific results (this helps you know you are on the right track). However, these effects/results remain the same. Throughout history, Mages have utilized the same techniques with cultural differences. I only reiterate what I can!

One should always understand the intended goal and use smudges accordingly to reach that goal. Use your intuition and speak with the energies of the incense in question. They will speak in kind to you!

Sage is a great "right now" Smudge, as is Cedar. However, as with many Earthly- plants, their clearing powers may only work on worldly matters, and much energy is universal. Smudging is effective in clearing a space of unwanted energy. They are of Earthly power! For example, a beginner or one who does not know may be affected by smudging. If they have extraordinary abilities, their energy may be denser; it is sometimes helpful to use a plant-metal-resin mixture to attain denser working.

Sage is excellent as a very light clearing during the Waxing moon. It may not be 100% and last for only a bit, yet the problem will continue to affect the things in question. Cedar is denser energy and can help against chaotic Earthly beings, most effectively used during a waning moon.

Any Plant may be used for smudge, lily, pine, marigold/calendula, etc. These listed are very common. It is of great benefit to use these in combination with others.

Resin scents cross energetic boundaries as they are both earthly and other/aiding in clearing universal energies. I have listed some of the most common.

FRANKINCENSE

extremely dense yet Light-Divine energy. This will bring in Divine powers to overcome the negative and clear. Frankincense is very solar energy. This is good to use in combination with almost any other incense.

MYRRH

This is a Dense yet, dark- or lunar energy. This also brings in many divine powers of differing sorts, dense and dark. These sacred energies will also help clear the space of negativity.

COPAL

It is its neutral energy as well. This is not only of Divine power but of Fey as well. This has no polarity- solar or lunar as it is neutral.

DRAGONS BLOOD

A dense resin, but it affects earthly and universal totems/energies. Dragon's Blood is mainly used in addition to other incense as it has great strength to add a power boost to what incense you are working with as it is multi-dimensional. It has a tremendous effect during the Waning moon/New moon period.

PINE

This resin does have many dense Earthly ties as it helps against or brings about totemic energies of this realm and others, depending on the mix and goal.

CINNAMON

This is a very positive, divine, healing solar scent. It attracts very comforting and wholesome energies. It has been used for that reason and is associated with the Samhain/Yule periods of the year.

CLOVE

A very positive yet dark lunar scent. This energy demands stillness and contemplation. The action only comes when things, peace, and reflection are attained. It is very effective against chaotic, confusing energies.

Multidimensional effects on all planes are created with the vibrational effects of metal!

I understand this is unusual, but through much theoretical physics study, I have learned this to be an easily accessible way to create lasting change. On a grand scale, I ask that one speak or commune with each metal, as each energy's details will be communicated.

IRON

The primarily used element does not harm anyone or faeries, as most people mistakenly believe. Iron is of the Earth so ask yourself why it would hurt anything but lousy energy. It is very grounding. By this, I mean it mainly is felt to resonate with the material realm and create the effect in Iron's unique way. Iron has been added to Incense to generate a charge of intended energy throughout realms, affecting them. So this is a _very_ extreme working/ incense. Well, it is no longer incense per se. It is now a functional spiritual element with material effects. Iron may be acquired in Iron ore, shavings/ Lodestone, Pyrite, Hematite and Magnets, and Boji Stones for their electrical impact on the material.

COPPER

Copper is easy to acquire. It is airy and spiritual in nature. Copper does have a higher vibration than Iron. It is recommended to work with Iron before copper, As iron absorbs all negative energy. Perhaps finish with copper, as it is an excellent conductor of all positive energy. One of the metals will create a spiritual/light/Divine vibration, primarily if used together once negativity is cleared.

LEAD

Please use caution when working with this!
Lead's charge is so unique that it holds or traps any current or previous livelihood energy. Therefore, lead may be used in any banishings or bindings one wishes to make permanent. Consider this wisely, for it will be endless! Lead can be found in fishing weights.

GOLD

A very conductive and resistant metal to solar/aggressive/ protective charge-vibration. This is used for adding charge/ vibration to a person or space. People enjoy wearing this for this purpose. Gold is found in either rose, white or yellow.

SILVER

Silver is the best conductor of electrically charged energy. Silver also reflects or sends back power to its immediate origin, cyclical. This metal people will adorn themselves with for these reasons.
Other ritual additions

GYPSUM/SULFUR,

Throw in flames for the electric blue effect! It also is a form of acquiring magical attention from Deities! Just be careful! Understand it stinks- It is a form of brimstone!

HIGH PROOF SPIRITS

Bacardi 151, or Ever clear, is a liquid used to create the Spirit Flame! One can, in a pinch, use Isopropyl alcohol!

An essential Draconic incense for use during basic circles or cleansing.

I will leave recipes for these different incenses in the recipe section of this book, and one should understand their basics.

MIRROR MAGICK

Mirrors are doorways to other realms and dimensions. Mirrors can be dangerous if misused. However, mirrors can be charged for specific reasons and can help us in many ways, Such as sending energy back to whence it came or radiating what power was sent.

Mirrors have been used for divination for many thousands of years. They take many forms, such as water, metal, or stone. A natural mirror will have much easier access to the Faery realm than a store-bought mirror. A mirror made by one's hand from natural items is the most potent above all.

A dark or black mirror is primarily used for Dark Crone or Dark Lord magick A mirror is always handmade. On the other hand, a light mirror will attract many spirits, and both types will attract many estranged entities. So I highly recommend one know their action before working this form of magick. Hence one may not wish to place a mirror in one's entryway. It is highly recommended to charge specific mirrors according to their use.

HUMAN MAGNETISM

Charisma, love & confidence are magnetic. Therefore, people flock to the person of Honor who wishes to attract these "young-minded" persons and give them a knowledgeable view of things they can use to enhance their lives!

People with a moral attitude and outlook on the proper "future" need to radiate this, for it may be confused as arrogance or wrongful pride. So please take a second look; these people are helping others and have magnetic personalities. However, a truly magnetic personality is not always just easily given. Sometimes we have to work for it.

To lead many in an honorable fashion, we must be like the "Pied Piper" and make others genuinely want to be around us. Leading by example, many people will come if we radiate love and caring with our charisma. If people fear approaching us, our love and caring help break the barrier!

WELL, THEN, WHAT IS A WASTE OF ENERGY!!

Suppose a person repeatedly allows destructive energy forces into their life and uses them to cause vengeance against others. When shown how things could be different, the destructive energy seemed gone. However, this same person kept allowing it back in (the bad energy). It is like an addiction. They want to get better but cannot.

It is easy and comfortable. However, once a person asks for help, many will not aid this continual self-destructive part of their lives. So one form of a waste of energy would be, trying to help someone or something that genuinely does not want it.

You can always tell by their refusal to listen to you or reverting to their self-destructive behavior.

WHAT ARE GODS CHILDREN

How Do I become God's child? What does this mean?? People get ousted unfairly for their differences and judged. Many questions are abounding about this, and many people from many walks and faiths will give their perspectives.

This perspective is shared and coincides with many other teachers with years of Spiritual Experience and Physical Experience. God is a name many paths will give to the Divine Creator, other traditions use many different names, but I will use "Divine" for all purposes.

ALL PEOPLE/BEINGS ARE ASPECTS OF THE DIVINE CREATION!!!

People need to understand, realize, and KNOW this as a fact! The Divine has created all things on this Earth, and we are a part of it. Thus, a Parent in no way expects their child to be disrespected, and a DIVINE being/person has the right to expect standards for themselves, meaning all of us !! It is not right to excuse the wrong person and allow them to hurt you again and again! That is disrespecting yourself and insulting the 'DIVINE.' You would not go into a Sacred Church of any sort and disrespect it. Hence harming yourself by allowing others to hurt you is the same DISRESPECT!

On the same note, as a part of the DIVINE, one also has a responsibility to all life by giving it basic respect! Basic respect is respect for all life/all people, whether a bully, murderer, or other. We all are on equal ground, and we cannot make a total judgment of a person because we disagree with their actions. Yes, morals will come to play much later, and respect is earned, but both are your personal decision on a deep level! First, however, a hurtful action must be taken into account.

The Divine will have a final decision about the life energy; for this reason, don't worry! So to sum things up, we and all beings are 'DIVINE' God's children, like it or not!

The best way to become God's Child is to lead by positive example. Not judging and being tolerant but defending/helping yourself and others in need.

MYSTICAL VIRTUES

Particular virtues cast Shamans, or Wise Ones, apart from the rest of secular society. We should keep these virtues in mind when dealing with each other in our everyday lives. Each virtue is the right way to behave in the realm of human functioning with which it is concerned. It is our benefit to function well in each Sphere of human activity, not because others will reward us or allow us to avoid punishment, but because it contributes to our eudemonia or "leading a flourishing life." Besides our fate, these virtues lead us to a deeper relationship with the Deities.

By consciously recognizing the different realms in which we act and choosing to function as well as possible in each domain, we will make ourselves stronger and wiser--more capable of avoiding bad things happening to us and responding constructively when they do. I will share these virtues. Love to all of you.

1. **Wisdom:**
   Sound judgment and the ability to perceive people and

situations correctly, deliberate about and decide on the correct response.
2. **Piety:**
Correct observance of ritual and social traditions, maintaining the agreements we humans have with the Gods and Spirits, and keeping the Old Ways through ceremony and duty.
3. **Vision:**
The ability to broaden one's perspective to have a greater understanding of our place/role in the cosmos, relating to the past, present, and future.
4. **Courage:**
The ability to be steadfast and appropriate in the face of danger.
5. **Integrity**:
Honor; being trustworthy to oneself and others, involving oath keeping, honesty, fairness, respect, and self-confidence.
6. **Perseverance**:
Personal Drive motivation to pursue one's goals even when that pursuit becomes difficult.
7. **Hospitality**:
Acting as both a gracious host and an appreciative guest, involving benevolence, friendliness, humor, and honoring a "gift for a gift."
8. **Moderation**:
Cultivating one's appetites so that one is neither a slave to them nor driven to ill health, mental or physical, through excess or deficiency.
9. **Fertility:**
Bounty of mind, body, and spirit, involving creativity, production of objects, food, works of art, and an appreciation of the physical.

CELTIC-GRECO ROMAN THOUGHT

In the times of Julius Caesar, the Celtic world is what we consider to be Pagan or with many Deities. However, the new Roman religion, Catholicism, was nonconforming to the Celtic/ Pagan thought pattern. A Celtic way of thought is very unified and cyclical **"I and nature are one"** is the 'philosophy used by the Celts. Nothing was questioned as evil, for evil was considered separateness of a duality the Celts did not understand. The entire universe had "good and evil," "positive and negative," For you cannot have one without the other.

The Celts looked at this 'Big picture' called the Earth-Universe and understood it as, let everything be, for if it was considered in balance and harmony with all, why fix it? The Celts also had this same view of themselves and how they learned. They did not write sacred knowledge for the general public, as the Christians did in the bible. The Druids felt very strongly that Sacred Knowledge comes from nature and within. If the Deities are willing to share knowledge and we are ready, they do so.

The Druids-Celts had difficulty understanding why to put Sacred Knowledge 'in a book.' they were an oral tradition. All Sacred Knowledge passed on was oral. Hence the debate of keeping a BOS/Grimoires is an 'interesting' rule. Many such things are called' Celtic Shamanism.' A real Celtic Shaman example would be the Druids. Many traditions have Shamans. Asatru are the Nordic Draconics of Germanic areas, Kahunas in the Hawaiian tradition, and Gnostics, the Christian Mystical shamans. Native American Medicine Men/Shamans, etc. Despite their practices, the Earth shares its traditional magic and dedicated paths.

The Celts believed their Deities personified all life's reverence and were sacred. Even after another's death, even an enemy of a Celt was revered as a Holy Being. Many would have you believe that the Celtic Druids practiced sacrifice just for sacrifice's sake. NO!! All life was sacred and ongoing. So giving life for life was understood as necessary, and promoting New Life!

Greco Roman

The thought pattern that is Greco-Roman is one that still exists today. Yet remember, the Romans during the Time of Caesar were at war with the Celts. Caesar had a very biased opinion about Celtic countries even though the peoples were much alike. The Greco-Roman religions and politics were ones of ascension and dualities. The Celtic cyclical balance of nature threatened the Greco-Roman thought- duality, so it was said to be spoiled and wrong. The dualities of evil and good, male and female, positive and negative, are essential to this system. The Celts do not understand these dualities as a natural expression of the universe.

Many Shamans love working with paradoxes/opposites! For example, nothing can be evil in Celtic thought, for the universe is all. However, an act that brings anything in the universe out of harmony on purpose may be called evil. In the Greco-Roman, though, 'nature is evil.'

So good folk must be against nature as far the Greco-Roman thought was concerned. The Celts always wondered and had trouble with "how" one can be against nature when Deity forms nature!

When you choose a pantheon, you decide what in your life you resonate with or respond to on a spiritual level. The separate Deities in these many pantheons help us bring out certain aspects of ourselves. So choose a pantheon to work with, one that has an energy that resonates with you, whether dualistic or balanced. All are learning experiences as we go along our path.

Norse examples would be Odin and Freja, God of Asgard and Goddess of love and Valkyries.

Celtic -British examples may be Cernunnos, lord of the hunt, Cerridwen, Goddess of Magic.

Irish examples may be Llugh, the sun king, and Danu, the Mother Goddess of the Irish people.

Welsh ex. May be Llew, god of the skilled hand, and Bloddeuwedd, Mother Goddess- Mesopotamian-Lilith.

Greek examples may be Artemis, the Goddess of the moon, hunting, and nature. Apollo, god of the sun, poetry, and music.

The Roman Dianna, Goddess of the Moon and hunt twin to Lucifer, god of the sun.

Children see deities also, in their way, as the two children who see the three sky gods and call "rain ghost" Odin, Thor, and Zeus.

Many Deities will decide they "like" to work with someone or resonate well with them and will let them know so through different experiences.

FAERY MAID OF ASTOLAT

<u>Adapted and expanded from A.L.Tennyson-
Lady of Shallot by A. Markham</u>

Camelot is surrounded by barley and rye fields that clothe the world and meet the sky. In this field is seen a road that runs by the many-towered Camelot. This road is traveled by many, being surrounded by luxurious beauteous lilies that blow in the wind. Over the silent isle below, the fragrant petals blow the island of Astolat. Many Willows and Aspens sway in the breeze surrounding the quiet island of Astolat, which embowers the fairy maid Elaine.

Elaine's castle is gray with four towers on this lone island, the highest of all. In this castle reside the Lord of Astolat and his daughter Elaine, the maid of Astolat.

Many pass this isle on barges of silken sail and the many horses on the road that lies across the river that leads to Camelot.

Do these many folks know of the fairy maid Elaine of Astolat? As to her name, none is definite. We can only be sure that men reaping barley in the fields on the river banks early in the morn' hear the echoes of a cheery, yet sad, but the sonorous tune. By the light of the moon, the reapers, weary of their days' work. Listen again to this beautiful tune and whisper to each other, "Tis, the fairy maid of Astolat."

By day and night, the maiden Elaine weaves a magical web of silken thread, using many bright and lovely hues. Alas, the maiden has heard the whispers of the wind. The language of the Sidhe, that ill-fated will she be if she lingers in this world by Camelot. The maid knows not what this ill fate may be. Hence she puts all thought into weaving her web, and little other care hath she. The Fairy maid of Astolat.

With the magical sight known only to the Faery Maid and her kind, the Sidhe, Elaine envisions many shadows of the world around her. With this Fairy sight, Elaine envisions the road winding down to Camelot and the many travelers upon it. The market girls in their red cloaks, a troupe of merry damsels, or perhaps a shepherd lad will pass on this road. On this road, too, may pass a long-haired page in crimson clad, or perhaps on the road, the Faery will envision Red Cross Knights riding two by two to the many-towered Camelot.

Greatly saddened by this is she, for Elaine hath no knight loyal and faithful will carry her favor.

The fairy maid of Astolat.

In the center of this small island of rolling hills is a mound, not unlike Tara, which lays the stronghold, the castle of Astolat. Among the four towers that belong to this castle lie Elaine's imbowerment. Her tower must be as tall or taller as the wide island, yet it is not as large a roundabout as the other three.

The web she weaves covers the whole of the tower, within and without. The fairy maid has built scaffolding at different tower heights to complete her weaving. She creates this as an actual web, for it becomes denser at the center from which the visions emanate. As the web fades out, so too do the images.

Elaine keeps weaving this web, matching the images of the world she envisions. But they constantly change; thus, the maiden is distraught, for she would like to see one complete image!

The Fairy maid Elaine weaves again at the bottom scaffold. When very weary, she falls into a magical sleep dreaming only of imperishable love. Thus as Elaine was stirring in her slumber. Many a bowshot awakened the fairy maid from her bower eaves. Elaine heard a rustling in the barley sheaves, and as she stated "Alas, what is this rustle I hear" the maid's eyes were blinded by a dazzling light shimmering through the leaves. The light emanated and appeared to be aflame upon the brazen greaves in which the light reflected itself. Kneeling before the maid, Elaine was a Red Cross knight, as was the figure upon his shield. This knight's bridle, dotted by many gems, shone free in the light like brilliant stars in the night sky.

As the knight rode in his luminated saddle, his armor chimed, and the bells from his harness rang a merry tune. This knight's broad, clear countenance in the sunlight glowed coal-black curls from under his helmet flowed as he sang a gay song riding through the bower eaves. Whence Elaine perceived this Red Cross knight from the many towered Camelot who was yet unknown to her.

The evening drew close, and the fairy maid approached the knight with an invitation from her father, the Lord of Astolat. Offering food and shelter for the eve was the custom in those chivalrous days. Elaine sat aside this Red Cross knight in the feasting hall, and in the merriment that followed the magnificent feast, Elaine learned that this knight intended to fight in a tournament at Camelot on the Morrow. While conversing with this knight, Elaine realized that this estranged cavalier was none other than the brave Sir Lancelot.

With this discovery, Elaine became enamored beyond human knowledge for this knight.

Thus Elaine asked the bold Sir Lancelot to wear her favor. But as Lancelot had already sworn love to another, he could not wear Elaine's favor and no other. So Lancelot refused the request, but at seeing Elaine's stricken look, he relented. Bearing Elaine's favor upon his crest would only add to his singular disguise.

Thus the noble Sir Lancelot rode onto the jousting field bearing upon his crest a scarlet scarf embroidered with many pearls. So the day rode on with the tournament proceedings. The alien knight, Sir Lancelot, proved to be successful throughout the day, albeit he did hazard a wound to his head as the day wore on.

On the eve, Sir Lancelot returned to the remote isle of Astolat, whence the fairy Maid Elaine nursed the wounded Sir Lancelot.

Months came and expired, and when Lancelot's vigor returned him, he seized an opportunity to express his gratitude to the Lord of Astolat and the Maiden Elaine for their tender care.

Thus as Sir Lancelot was preparing to take his leave, the Maiden Elaine tried vainly to detain him by her many tears and solicitations of love. She watched the object of her affections depart. Finally, without leaving her any hope, Lancelot told Elaine that his heart was given to another. Thus he returned home to Camelot. Many months had come and gone since Lancelot's departure. Thus the vigor and strength of the fairy maid gradually sunk. Elaine felt that she could not live without the object of her affection any longer.

So the Maid left the web, the room, then the Castle, and down she came to the banks of Astolat. Descending the river brink, she found a barge beneath a Willow and among the Water Lilies. This Barge Elaine loosed from its moorings; she stepped inside and set adrift towards Camelot.

Many Red Cross knights spied this barge on the shores of Camelot. It held a maiden robed in snowy white and holding a scarf upon her breast. The Red Cross knights knew this scarf, notably sir Lancelot, who knew this maiden well. Pursuing his search in the barge, Sir Lancelot discovered a purse richly embroidered with gold and jewels. Within it was a letter addressed to him stating Elaine's love for Lancelot, the most beautiful of men and the most accomplished of knights! Stating too how the cruel love produced her to lose vigor and wan. Written by the hand of the Fairy Maid Elaine of Astolat.

Lancelot sadly buried her with all honors suited to her rank. With much regret, he stated

"She hath a lovely face. God, in his mercy, lends her grace, The Fairy Maid Elaine of Astolat"

ENERGY AND SPIRITUAL EVOLUTION

It is necessary to understand when someone uses a word such as Dragon, Angel, or Faery. These people use human terms to describe the differences in Universal Energy, whether they know it or not. This is done so that most people may have difficulty believing it and they can understand the discussed subject. The physical forms these energies take also represent what humans understand. Many people feel separate energy around them and wonder at its existence! It is not different energy -It is a part of your own!! One can learn from this through meditation and quietly speaking with your spirits! I will explain this energy that is felt as best I can, which may help you understand your feelings.

This is a complicated subject to address, as many others are not prepared to discuss or even understand vibrational energies.

Unfortunately, many people mistakenly think that learning the physical sciences negates the spirituality many of us accept. However, much in science and mysticism are still being discovered and explained by each other in different ways.

These sciences help, for example, Quantum physics, which a person should begin to study! Chemistry, Electromagnetism, Astrophysics, Biology, and the many forms of earth and life sciences give generous alms to what many know of in spiritual terms, for they illustrate. visually and verbally that which I write and help instruct.

In Physics, energy is the capacity to do work. For example, the Quantitative property must be transferred to an object to perform work on or heat the item. Energy is a conserved quantity; energy conservation law states that energy can be converted but not created or destroyed.

Mystically, energy is a vibration many others can sometimes understand yet, must experience to relate to. However, energy is NOT something that can be manifested materialistically, only attracted for much of it genuinely can only exist in differing dimensions.

Before I begin, let me say that otherworldly/etherical beings' energy should entail just that! These attitudes, philosophies, and feelings should strive to embody one human life. Work with these lessons as they may be understood and taught to and by you. These energies may change in vibration, but the physical beings embodied by these energetic forms exist in another dimension that we **can** both see and hear.

Do not try to manifest these beings in a human form. Many of these high vibrational beings cannot manifest in the human realm/ dimension; they are very complex, and their energy is too dense. The third dimension we live in does not allow etherical beings to exist, only energetic vibrations of specific types. Do not be disheartened! The human words I use to describe these differing energies/beings are the only way to tell people must understand these exist in other dimensions beyond the third dimension of all humans. Please be happy with that. A person who **can see** intuitively will understand what another person's soul level may be on. No energy is better than another, and the final incarnations -Angelic, Draconic, even Complex Fey- may differ.

Each individual is capable of aligning with their energetic evolution to move forward. All forms of manifestation and the lessons needed to be learned **must not** be skipped. That would be like jumping from a baby to an adult- **foolish!** It is a Universal law that advancement/growth happens. Quantum physics has shown us that through the expansion and complexity of the universe! It is not wise for a person to stop this and acts as they wish. That stagnation angers many Spirits and the Universe as well. Even those beings we refer to as Deities are in another dimension advancing as they will. Have you noticed Lilith or Ogma, for example, feel denser and energetically alive than previous people have ever recorded? Are they advancing? Yes!! Remember, this process takes many, many thousands of years.

For in all the varying incarnations, in all dimensions/realms, a person will have the same lessons repeated with more wisdom to apply on a universal level. The lessons taught in each incarnation are the same, yet we learn to be more creative and wiser in overcoming these challenges/lessons and, eventually, complete the learning!

Loki is one of many Deities who are great teachers. Any Trickster! Many Deities help all people address these same lessons and overcome them. In overcoming this, people may realize that they are more durable than they give themselves credit for and can resolve their challenges. Loki is a Trickster spirit that helps us learn this; that is his mischief!

All people have a beginning to their Soul/Spirit- A new soul (if you will) usually is unsure, energetically confused, or chaotic- that is normal. These people (on our plane) have a soul age equivalent to a human newborn to a toddler. Many people find this to be annoying, as children sometimes are. They seem not to care much and can be very closed or materialistic. There is no caring about spirituality as a whole. An essential starting point, many new souls, do have empathy, but it is misplaced.

A new soul responds to many aspects of energy that have a higher vibration. Fey is a universal natural Energy effortless for all to understand. Draconic, or Angelic beings, are denser and much more complex others choose not to like the complexity they feel. These new Spirits/beings are trying to decide which resonates with or feels more comfortable. Destiny from the Universe also plays a hand in this well. These beginners may be new souls and will advance only when all their lessons are completed and their souls develop.

This is a process for all that will easily take many lifetimes. When this is complete, a person will only advance/evolve spiritually to the next energy/ vibrational level. Yes, an order is expected, as in school grades and graduation. However, a person may encounter a mature child, the most common form. This person is growing and will continue with their lessons when mature enough in human form to move on. Many high vibrational beings, such as Draconic or Angelic, being misinterpreted as Fey, are an energy everyone can easily understand.

One can tell an old soul for the child seems wiser than their years and more comfortable in Spiritual silence.

SIMPLE FAERY

This is one of the first energetic transformations of a soul. This energy is equivalent to a human toddler or young child. It is beautiful to many, quickly resonates with them, and attractive to many. These beings can be identified in the human realm by an abundance of song, dance, or music. This energy loves life- either in plant or animal form. All SimpleFaery is very obsessive about activism. Almost to absurd lengths. Unfortunately, being driven is present in the people in this vibration. They could care less about The importance of the enormous picture energy, universal messages, divine energy, and grand universal concepts that make The Divine or the universe easier to understand. These concepts are too complex for a simple faery to comprehend: This energy understanding and vision are very tunneled and focused on one thing.

COMPLEX FAERY

This energy signature understands the need for all balance. Male/female, animal/plant, universal/earthly, energies, and needed. This being loves experimentation in working with other realms and realities. This energy is beginning to understand the need for chaos, suffering, and disorder in nature's spirits, governing a specific aspect of the natural world. This vibration can be as simple as a love for life in its many forms! This may be the purest form of Fey energy to which one can relate. A new step in transitioning like this is known to be experienced by many. One will be able to work with and understand how destiny plays a role in their life and how one can work with it. A soul will spend many lifetimes learning the same lessons but with a more sophisticated understanding. The ideas, thoughts, and philosophies will change and be understood by these people in a more complex manner than before.

The people in this incarnation period begin working with other realms and realities. This means understanding the need for chaos, suffering, and evil. After completing the Simple Faery, the complex Faery vibration/presence typically comes in many lifetimes. Finally, all these vibrations' lessons are repeated to learn more complex wisdom.

DARK FEY

Not all people experience this vibration. Dark Fey is part of an individual's chosen spiritual destiny.

A very dark fey, for they are, with much knowledge of Dark magic. Not blood-sucking-garlic hating like storybooks and movies would have us believe. There are many examples of Dark Fey. Such as the Unseelie court. Selkies and many others. Many dark Fey who seem to be cursed by other high vibrational energies fall into this category and are very misunderstood.

Many Vampire qualities are human-made myths. However, this Dark Fey does love the dark, night, and winter.

Vampires have many degrees of evolution as well and do not all fit in one category -do not try to make them all fit together! And once again, I state- Do not try to manifest this being in the third dimension, making you look foolish! If a Fey chooses to appear to you or any form, they are generally seen in the third and half dimensions (3-1/2). Humans can see many spirits discussed here in this dimension; however, they may be seen out of (the corner of your eye) or with a very soft gaze. Their opposite would be an Angelic being.

DEATH WALKER

These beings are lovely and have many ties to the realm of the dead and even demonic realms as guardians. They work best here and understand what many may think of as evil. These people resonate with and follow an aspect of complex dark faery yet with the dead's energy if you wish. Their vibration is very hard to distinguish as upbeat and lively or dead and dark as they do not respond to life as we know it.

Please allow yourself to advance spiritually! However, do not insult others for their lack of knowledge! That is detrimental to your physical and spiritual happiness!

SUBTERRANEAN BEING

A person with this energy almost feels Demonic; these people have a gross evil feeling but only seem to ingest and destroy life. On the other hand, a Subterranean being does not have the Divine/Sinful nature of a Demon; they destroy life because they can; if a Subterranean being has one in its sights, it will never rest until it fully harms that life. Hence many rituals in this book can help with this. The Subterranean is another level that humans can evolve to, nothing more.

ANGELIC BEINGS

A person of high vibration has evolved over thousands of lifetimes through all transformations discussed here. They work with and assist Draconic Beings with a person's emotional level. The people who have grown to this level naturally interpret Divine messages no matter the tradition. They may follow the Divine themselves and listen to others in need. They have a natural and, many times, mystical understanding of Divine messages, strength, and healing. These people help people mainly heal their emotions and help others bring aspects of Divine knowledge into their personal lives. Angelic Beings help over the powers of the emotional body and mind. They quickly refer to many Sacred words for all, depending on necessity. They are the universal warriors, healers, and messengers, and Michael is their Universal Angelic/Draconic leader of the Divine Host/warriors. He is both Angel and Dragon.

Just as Dragons/Draconic beings cannot exist in the human realm, neither do Angel/Angelic beings. They work and assist Dragons, for the two are complete equals. However, the difference between

Dragons and Angels is that an Angel works and helps many people on an emotional/soul level and manifests balance emotionally in one's life. A Dragon/Draconic being affects the physical life of a person. These beings have surpassed all vibrations known to man and do not exist in the human realm.

DRACONIC BEING

Also, a person of extremely high vibration has evolved over thousands of lifetimes through all transformations discussed here. They work with and assist Angels. A Dragon has a very high yet dense vibration. This will make many feel very heavy and not want to do anything new. However, this is an energy a person must get used to, for there is much on the Earth to coincide with.

These people are naturally inclined towards any of the sciences or legal careers. Their predisposition is to help others empower themselves physically. As they work closely with the Angelic, they naturally know who a person may get additional advice from, aid, and help physically, bringing physical manifestation into those they help. Dragons have surpassed all forms of vibration known to man and no longer exist in the human realm. An example of dense energy is a haunting feeling that may cause sadness or confusion. Paradoxes are a constant with these beings, and a person following this path may efficiently work with paradoxes. The best way I can describe a contradiction is when you feel you are going forward in time- yet the past is being relieved simultaneously. These Dragons/Draconics always help on the materialistic/physical plane, unlike the Angels/Angelics who help on the emotional plane.

SENSITIVES/NORNS

Humans who see and feel Draconic/Angelic beings' vibrations interpret them as wise teachers for others in the human realm. Norns are mischievous/trickster Fey spirits. They were named for the oldest Faeries! A person who is a Norn is not only in love with life in a complex way but also loves death as the Dark Fey. These may be called Norns. The Norn in myth is the oldest form of faery. They are somewhat rare, and this knowledge they give and possess CAN NOT be taught in any incarnation. They are an addition to any spiritual aspect of one's living. Loki is a dark fey. Norn A Norn is famous for causing mischief in the form of giving people tests that the person has the capability of surpassing. That person does not remember that lesson. A Norn helps one remember. They are associated and known to work with spiders; all weaving of life don't remember how! A Norn Deity will send us these tests.

"How do I know what spiritual manifestation/incarnation I am living?"

You know more than you think! To answer this question, ask yourself what your personality is like. The traits of each incarnation are given here through the many incarnations we go through. Are you an activist for plants/animals? Do you like Divine knowledge? Work with/Understand the balance and chaos of life? Do you enjoy sarcasm or working with your hands? Are you a nerd who loves science? All of these beings in the spiritual realm have these human traits. However, many people are afraid to let themselves spiritually advance, which annoys many. Do be honest with yourselves.

There are many details of these incarnations and too many to cover.

DRACONIC PHILOSOPHIES AND UNDERSTANDINGS

STRENGTH

MARGARET READ MACDONALD-BOY SCOUT TROOP.COM
A STORY FROM THE LIMBE PEOPLE OF WEST AFRICA

The animals decided to have a contest to see who was the strongest. This contest was Elephant's idea.
"Everybody meet on Wednesday. We'll see who has STRENGTH."
The first to arrive was Chimpanzee.
A Chimpanzee came in, jumping around.

"Strength-I've got strength. See these ARMS! Just wait till they see my strength!"
Chimpanzee sat down.

Deer arrived.
"Strength! Look at these LEGS! I have such strength."
Deer sat down.

Next came Leopard. Leopard was showing his claws and growling. "Strength! Look at these CLAWS! I... have STRENGTH!"
Leopard sat down.

In came bushbuck. Bushbuck lowered his strong horns. "Strength! See these horns! This is strength." Bushbuck sat down.

Elephant came in. Elephants move slowly. "El...e...phant... means strength". Elephant sat down. They waited, And waited, One more animal to come. They waited more.

At last, Man came running in. "STRENGTH! STRENGTH!" Man was showing off his muscles. "Here I am! We can START now!"

Man had brought his gun to the forest. Man had been hiding his gun in the bush. That is why he was late. Elephant took charge.

"Now that Man is finally here; we can begin. Chimpanzee, Show us strength."

Chimpanzee jumped up. He ran to a small tree and climbed it. He bent it over and tied it in a knot. He climbed back down. "Strength! Was that STRENGTH?!! What strength!"

The animals cheered. "Strength! Strength! Strength! Strength! THAT'S strength!" The animals calmed down.

"Well...Chimpanzee, SIT DOWN. Who is next?"

Deer leaped up. Deer ran three miles into the forest. Then, Deer ran three miles back. Deer wasn't even out of breath. "There! Wasn't that strength!"

The animals agreed. "Strength! Strength! Strength! Strength! That was STRENGTH!"

"Well... Deer, SIT DOWN. Who's next?"

Leopard leaped up. Leopard drew out his long claws. He began to scrape at the Earth.

Scrung...scrng...scrung...scrung...

The dirt just flew! The animals jumped back.
They were frightened. "Aaah!"
"Wasn't that strength?
"Strength! Strength! Strength! Strength! Strength!
That was STRENGTH!"

"Well... Leopard, SIT DOWN. Who's next?"

Bushbuck was next. Bushbuck lowered his massive horns. A cane field was there. Bushbuck began to plow through that cane field. *Shuuu... shuuu... shuuu... shuuu...*
His horns just made a ROAD right through that field. Bushbuck turned around. *Shuuu... shuuu... shuu... shuuu...* he plowed a road right back. "WASN'T THAT STRENGTH?"
"Well... Bushbuck, SIT DOWN. Who's next?"

Now came Elephant. Many trees were there. They were growing close together. The elephant leaned his massive shoulder against those trees. *Eeennhh... eeennhj... eeennhh... kangplong*!
Those trees fell fight over. "STRENGTH! Was THAT strength?!"
Well... elephant, SIT DOWN!. Who's next?"

Man's turn. Man ran to the middle of their circle. Man started whirling around. He turned somersaults, and He turned cartwheels; he did handsprings. That man was twirling all over the place. Man stopped. "Strength! Strength! Wasn't That STRENGTH?!"
THE animals looked at one another. "Well... that was exciting."
"But... was it strength?"
"Not really..."Is that all you can do?"

Man was insulted. "Well then, watch THIS?" Man climbed to the top of a palm tree *So fast! So fast!* He threw down palm nuts. He climbed back down again. "Strength! Strength! Was that strength?!"
The animals looked at him. "Would you call that strength?" He just climbed a tree. That's not really strength. Is there anything else?"
Man was ANGRY. "Strength? I'll show you STRENGTH!" Man ran into the bush. He grabbed his gun. He ran back again Man pointed his weapon at Elephant.

Ting...
He pulled the trigger. *Kangalang*!
Elephant fell over. Dead.   Dead.
Man was jumping and bragging. "Strength! Strength! Wasn't THAT strength?!"

Man looked around. The animals were gone. They had fled into the forest. "Strength!"
There was no one left to hear him brag.
Man was alone.

In the forest, the animals huddled together and talked. "Did you see that?"
"Was that strength?"
"Would you call that strength?"
"NO, that was DEATH"
"That was DEATH."

Since that day, the animals will not walk with man. So when Man enters the forest, he has to walk by himself.

The animals still talk of Man, That creature, Man... He is the one who cannot tell the difference between strength.... and Death.

SHADOW WORKING

What is it, and why is it important? Many teachers/people assume others know what or why Shadow working is essential. So one must confront the darker aspects of themselves that attract negative energy. These confrontations help the person learn how to understand and possibly get rid of this negative energy. Such stress from their jobs leads to unhappiness, hate, and meditation through negative energy. They know how to assimilate the positive qualities and focus on the negative aspects of your life. Such as depression or grief. It is essential or a person to understand what Shadow working is and why it is crucial. Most people require this and may need instruction on this process. Therefore, I will pass it on to you. Shadow working is essential when you have an insurmountable amount of chaos/stress and wish to organize it! This process communicates and validates your life's necessary emotions or aspects. It also expresses the many chaotic or damaging parts of your life. SHADOW WORKING will communicate the processes to heal these aspects and organize them.

The easiest method is Tarot divination, or what makes you comfortable to listen to the spirits. But I know people are different and are comfortable with various tools. So ask plainly in your thoughts before the tarot reading begins " Help me understand what is currently going on in my life at present and very near future." People may learn of many things currently happening in their lives that require work/attention.

Plus, how activities involving me may turn out if I do not change my thought patterns- making self-healing a priority. This is where SHADOW WORKING helps you! I highly recommend the book **TAROT SHADOW WORK** by Christine Jette. This information will help one delve into methods to heal themselves.

Writing, journaling, and putting your feelings on paper are significant components. First, get your emotions out!!! This is a tactic that allows you to release your thoughts peaceably. Then, reread what you wrote- are there any additions to the actions you wish to make? Maybe what do you feel you need to do/or not do? This component allows you to understand and see what is presently in your thoughts.

Another positive component is physical activity of some sort. This is a socially acceptable, peaceable way of getting your emotions with a physical action- not fighting!! As I know, most feel like they want to do it! Whether it be working out, yard work, cleaning, or whatever strenuous activity you choose. Get that excess physical energy out! Many people find these relaxing activities to allow their creative minds to flow. Whether coloring, drawing, constructing, puzzles- anything that allows creativity to flow. This allows your mind to relax and communicate calmly with you.

You find many things you could exchange, such as arguing- and replacing it with- realizing that not all arguments are worth the waste of energy/ yet do not allow someone to be verbally abusive to you. Stand up for yourself! Realize you are worthy of good things!! Do this creative mental relaxation technique regularly. It dramatically helps ease your mind- again, I say- It communicates peaceably to you. This gives you a sense of real accomplishment that you are capable of beauty.

Shadow working IS a continual process, and many components may become part of your life! So do not be afraid to embrace working with your darker shadow side or grief. A person needs to understand what Shadow is and why it is crucial Talk to those who have done this, for they know. Respect is given to those who ask for help when needed- a person must lose their pride; humility is a great lesson! Utilize dark deities to aid in this; they will guide you on your path!

SHADOW WORKING is not the complicated process some tell you it is, and I wish you success on your journey through this!

<u>FORGIVE AND FORGET</u>

People tell you to "Forgive and Forget,'" but a natural, healthy attitude of this is not easy to acquire. Why forgive? Do we truly forget? How does one let go? It is moving beyond the terrible wrong that has been done to you. Do not allow this to take over your thoughts! Move beyond this negativity and concentrate on living your life. Psychologists will tell you to let go, but we never forget as people. So don't try to brainwash yourselves with the whiny "Godlike" excuse people tell you: forgiving is normal because it is just an excuse for allowing stupidity to thrive!

In a previous message, I stated we are all Divine Creations-well being God's Children, we are!!! Hence, as a Divine Creation, we must not disrespect ourselves by allowing hurtful actions or people into our lives!!! The Divine would not ask us to be so unreasonable!!!

However, we must learn to "Let go," which is a synonym for forgiveness!

By Forgiving, you are taking that hurtful feeling in your gut and transferring it back to the person who gave it to you! FOR they hurt you-GIVE them back the responsibility of dealing with the pain! FOR-GIVE!!

Forgiveness is done with much prayer or visualization of you taking this action that makes sense to YOU!! Forgiveness is a challenging process and may take a while. You, however, do NOT need to allow the same hurtful person into your life again!!! Give the anger back to the person's energy that wronged you! THAT is normal, People change and learn, but this also takes years!! Give them years to do so! Remember, you are Divine Beings- Responsible and whole! Don't let anyone tell you otherwise! The offense still occurred, but as people, we all make mistakes, and after a time, you may allow the person-being that wronged you to be active in your life again! But that is up to you! However, you can reasonably–not forget but put it behind you and move on with your life.

GROUNDING AND CENTERING

The purpose behind grounding and centering is not discussed as much as I would like, for many assume one understands why this is done. However, grounding is excellent for bringing one's energy to the earth plane/grounding for whatever endeavor we embark on. This is important as we are part of the Earth and need to unite with its energy.

This will bring us more success as our intuitions awaken with this action. They are more sensitive as they are awakened in the earthly realm.

When one centers themselves, what is mainly meant is bringing in and gathering one's energies, so they are not making you feel scattered and frazzled." Gathering your energies and building a protection field with grounding is part of the grounding exercise. You may see areas of light uniting and radiating from you, scattered as they may be.

Focus on your thoughts, internalize them, and focus on your space. Your auric space is sacred and protective. Listen to the trees or the music. Etc. Feel and open your senses to nature and notice the rhythm of the elements around you.

Realize you are part of the energies and become one with them as you partake in their joy.

You can use a spectral visualization; however, nature is most comfortable, practical, and barefoot. Many like music, walks, and Graveyard walks are excellent!

Writing and rituals are done at your pace, to your liking. Do not forget the healing of candlelight, especially Himalayan salt candles. Salt of any sort helps, as well as incense, as does any action that puts your mind at ease. During your sleep, listening to relaxing music, anything over 400hz/hertz aids spiritual healing.

GRIEF AND UNDERSTANDING IT

Grief is normal and natural, yet many people think it is unimportant or even effortless to overcome. Grief can be overcome, but takes time, grounding, and shadow working is necessary for this healing. Mainly for fear of the unknown or becoming depressed and not knowing what to do. The Random House dictionary defines grief as Mental suffering over affliction or loss. There are many losses, and some are easier to overcome than others. However, sharp sorrow and painful regret are often endured alone or in silence.

Why do people do this to themselves? Well, grief is a normal and appropriate emotional response to a loss! For example, one person's pet may be as important to another person's child, spouse, or friend. Grief is about change, a change has abruptly come to your life, and it takes time for your heart and mind to handle it emotionally. It could take several months or years, but one never seems to forget. The bad days of grief become fewer and fewer over the following months/year, but they will occur. This, too, is normal.

Never feel guilt over the loss of someone or something, as part of guilt implies an intent to harm (to yourself mostly) emotional harm, and ask yourself the actual cause of this pain-reflect on it, ask yourself. Are you addicted to this feeling? Do you believe you deserve to feel this way? That is not beneficial for growth and change. Hidden within some feelings, one may wish things had been different or better. That, too, is very normal. When you write a letter to your loved one discussing your feelings, these feelings may signal.

If you analyze those relationships, you will live those dreams and let your loved one live through you, either through their favorite clothes, actions, or places. Honorably live as you feel best. Yet it is normal for everyone to have regrets, for not everything is perfect- so do not "Beat yourself up!" However, one must not keep reliving their grief, creating guilt, and never dwell on the past. Instead, remember to acknowledge what has happened, for the only emotions that cannot change are those that are not accepted.

Do NOT try to fool yourself into believing that things are better. This may make things much worse. How well you recover and heal is not the same as dwelling on the loss. Dwelling on a loss is a massive pitfall that can even last many years.

Think of others-
One must set an example for others; it is psychological to heal yourself first, for you will do others no good if you do not heal. Plus, it helps children understand what is okay to learn as well. As a feeling response, "I was very angry with the world." Because of the loss- I wanted to yell, "I hurt!!" DO IT! Yell and scream – in an uninhabited area, of course!! Never act unfairly and selfishly to others. Especially if they did nothing to hurt you, it would be best to put yourself in check, and I remind others to do the same. Being angry is a natural thing- don't take it too far.

Stay active-
Activity helps one focus on moving on with life-yet be careful not to ignore it. It is okay to remember the loss. Stone Healings, Reiki, Rites of Release, or offerings to the deceased person help communicate with their spirit, and we know it is okay to move on. A great teacher who WILL understand and share pearls of wisdom with you is the Angel of Death- AZRAEL. This ANGEL is known as the Grim Reaper or Hades, Lord of the Underworld, Keeper of the Dead.

A genuine spiritual connection with a loved one does not make the grieving process easier but more bearable. Once a real spiritual connection is made between people beyond the physical communication in life. Inter-dimensionally allows communication, and communication with loved ones is much easier to access and perform. This makes the passing and grieving more bearable.

Celebrate the passing of someone; celebrate their life! Accompany your mourning/grief. It will make their death much easier on you and create the spirit of-? Happy that you are getting along fine without them. Grief is an emotional, not an intellectual, part of life. Joy always helps a person heal, as in Wakes, or any celebrations of life, have fun, have a party - celebration!! Grief comes in waves and is not linear; if so, it would be challenging for us to handle it- the energy knows! There are many stages of grief. In denial, a person may be angry with the deceased, thinking, "Why did you leave me?" or bargaining.

The person may tell themselves, "I will do this, and the problem will begin to go away," and, hopefully, accept the loss. There are no time frames for this healing experience; remember, **time** does not necessarily heal, but **action** does!! Try not to compare losses, for they all are different and experienced differently. Perhaps nothing is responsible for the loss. Remember, this is a process; try to find an excellent spiritual/ emotional action for you!!! It is a good idea to stay active, work out, and use the stresses of life to give you strength in your workout. Coloring, sewing, and writing are helpful methods of relaxing your mind and making the most of your healing time.

Notice how you listen to others, for listening to others tell their stories helps one cope with life changes and makes these much more accessible, thus healing. Be an active listener, and articulate what the other person has told you and your intuitive observations. You do not need to help; you must sit and listen. Many people do not want a savior but a listener. Please don't compare your problems, for they cannot be the same. Telling one's own story helps them come to terms with and not live in denial.

LISTENING

The hurt individual will form a subculture and rebel if they feel ignored. Remember, changing your attitude from depression to more optimism will help change one's outlook on life. Talk to anyone, write and share, and socialize with others.

CLEANSING YOUR PHYSICAL LIVING AREA

People find this an annoying task, and some seem to be very picky, for a good reason. Many need to create order out of chaos/disorder, for chaos breeds more chaos! Some people get angry or can not think straight as long as confusion exists in their living space. With this chaos surrounding them, anger and disorganized thought may occur in some individuals. They may "feel" the chaotic and damaging energy around them. The existence repulses them- as they have it in their control to fix this and take appropriate action. The power attracted by the pestilence and disorder only attracts more of the same. YUK!!!

Negative energy will always be attracted to chaos, verbal or physical fights, laziness, a careless attitude to life, or even bugs and pests. Keeping something clean and orderly is a physical form of repulsing negative energy, which tries to come in all shapes in our lives-without it, there would be no positive and growth energy. Cleansing makes room for this growth and allows positive energy to abound. Yes, it is very accurate that some beings are impervious to the energy shift and have no problems with either one, but this must be carefully understood as the pros and cons are a balance of the two.

There may, however, be a personality trait that must be attended to. However, that is another topic addressed elsewhere.

DIS/ABILITIES

These are abundant in the general public and should never be taken for granted. Those with dis/abilities have many gifts that may be unknown. Yet, for the longest time, it has been the norm of many to tell the populous of us with dis/abilities about what they CAN NOT do. That is sooo wrong! Those with dis/abilities may have to work harder in certain areas, but they are not useless.

My and my son's disability is epilepsy, and I recount my many learnings over the past 50 years. At a very young age, I was given severe neurodepressants. Later in life, I learned to interpret the things I experienced. I had been taking harsh drugs and understood I would have intense hallucinations. But this also leaves my mind open to radical spiritual visions or messages. I, however, DO NOT recommend this as a standard practice. Never take these visions too literally, for spiritual understanding is very spherical! I have witnessed many people with differing dis/abilities have differing abilities outside the spectrum of what many consider normal.

It airs almost as if nature is taking- something natural- away and showing us how to utilize a different aspect of natural self-ability: blind, cerebral palsy, autism, and many others. Yet, I have witnessed those afflicted have astounding spiritual skills.

Yet, again this should never be overinterpreted or taken lightly, like a person who tries to find meaning in EVERYTHING they experience! This is not beneficial. Previously past generations have attempted to treat us as "INCAPABLE," which is very wrong; I have been told that as an epileptic, I would have inadequate coordination and be deficient in school/unintelligent. I cannot operate machinery and rely on medications for everything, have bad health, and rely on others to help me. STUPID!!! I can understand complex subjects naturally, and I am an honor student. I have many awards. Others have the same excellent abilities, I am sure of it! Everyone's powers are different and ever-changing.

Many friends and I have been spoken to with old-fashioned beliefs. We were told people with epilepsy did not have the clarity of mind to care for themselves. We were unintelligent; that is very WRONG!!! Knowing what was best for our situation was not even considered a possibility. Many people have to rely on others to get care

A person understands their own body better than anyone else! Many controlling people try to make those with Disabilities reliant on others. I knew this to be false, needing to be done when necessary, like those who are incapacitated. I kept a mental note of all information I could pass on to others at a young age.

Realize the Disabilities. We are supposed not to be innovative. However, many naturally have a higher average IQ and are more talented than expected in certain areas, like memory. We all have these blessings in disguise, and we all, with dis/abilities, know our bodies and talents best!! However, I must warn against using any ability or Dis/ability as an excuse for a person to be cocky or arrogant or even as an excuse not to act. That is never good in any aspect!!! Many of us have either the ability to see, hear, or many other skills, and negative comments/criticisms should only be taken with a grain of salt. Human nature is a lot stronger than we are given credit for.

SUFFERING

Many people do not like witnessing suffering, finding it offensive or evil. Yet, it is an essential part of life, Just as death is a tragedy, but a part of life. Suffering is not evil but is a very dark, misunderstood energy. Dark deities rule this energy. Be they Loki, the Norns, Death/Arawn, or many others. Suffering is a part of life, but people need to experience suffering as a reminder that they are always stronger than they give themselves credit for.

Suffering reminds many human beings that they have the ability and strength to overcome their problems and threatening situations. Human innovation and wit are necessary to overcome sadness, and many people do not practice these skills. The easy path many choose is to become passive and fearful. They portray the "victim" in action and thought. Many give in to unfortunate circumstances and fear rather than fight suffering head-on.

Becoming aware and proactive with oneself and helping others do so is a great start! Sharing information on how to overcome problems is essential and sends good, positive energy. Many resist the tragedy of Suffering. But many people want to force them to become passive-and embrace the 'Victim" idea. That is not very beneficial!

Suffering truly affects the strong of character as they witness this tragedy and try to aid others in overcoming their unfortunate situations and others' suffering. Many beings understand this is a part of life. The strength and positive energy humans have CAN overcome many forms of torture. It is unfair to force others not to give in to fear, darkness, anguish, or despair. It is hard for many. These people choose to accept the passivity and illusion of safety. The choice to fight against suffering and overcome belongs to all.

SELF HEALING

Despite what anyone says or does to help heal you, be it laying on hands, stones, Reiki, or energy healing, one needs to practice healing themselves to be most effective, self-sufficient or empowered. There are several ways to do this, and they are not flashy but highly typical. I never thought about it by most as healing techniques.

One's problems always stem from the chakras; if one is imbalanced spiritually in a Chakra Center, one will be imbalanced physically. Helping oneself is the least hurtful and self-empowering method as most healings can be. Free will is always involved in the self-healing process. Remember, this takes much time, so do not expect miracles overnight. Many healing techniques here have chakra exercises and tools that can help.

Root Chakra

Imbalance signs
Very seriously lacks humor or is too airheaded/airy

Self-help Techniques walking around a graveyard puts you in touch with the underworld energies, hiking, gardening, and anything done with the Earth regularly.

The Seat of Life/Sacral

Imbalance signs
Usually, an imbalance in your sexual drive for more or less little or much passion.

Self-help techniques
Swimming or spas, abstain from or make Love a lot. True Love Utilize tantra and yoga if you can.

Manipura/Solar Plexus

Imbalance signs
Codependency, addictions of sorts- too passive or too aggressive.

Self-help Techniques
Work on assertiveness, do handwork, write, cook, and dance, which helps all chakras, mainly this one.

Anahata-heart

Imbalance signs
Lack of or too much unreasonable empathy. Lack of romantic love, fierce love only! Too selfish or selfless.

Self-help Techniques
Find Love romantic or perfect Love of a friend, and it matters not. Write healing love notes, especially to yourself. Love yourself, and write affirmations. Find what you love and do it/carpe diem.

Vishudda-vocal creativity

Imbalance signs
Lack of or fear of speaking up or expressing yourself in words, expressing yourself too much, and not listening to others.

Self-help techniques

Practice anything vocally, reciting, singing or chanting, and speaking different languages. If you need to temper your self try communicating with American Sign Language.

Ajna-spiritual-visual-creativity

Imbalance signs

Over interpretation of the mundane world, hallucinating, to headaches and confusion.

Self-help techniques

Visualizing or imaginative thought daily, meditating with these visualizations, and then progress, watching anything you find beautiful from sunset to art and walking through a beautiful area, interpreting symbols and drawing of all sorts.

Sahasrara-crown

Imbalance sign

Too airy, when one thinks their information or knowledge is only the right way or constantly questions what they know. Spiritual control freak.

Self-help techniques

Writing to the Divine on all levels, or babbling away, so what! Studying subconscious symbols-mythology- symbology opens your mind. Practice the art of divinatory tools, and open the door. Listen to classical music. Drawing and chanting ritually are excellent for many chakras.

CHAKRA MANTRA CHARTS

There are many healing methods. The Chakras, qualities details, and Mantras help with certain yoga positions. I have found- when I am alone. I do not need a ceremonial ritual. Doing a small personal practice with the mantras and meditations may be enough! Use your creativity/intuition. Use your intuition for your detailed learning. Trust yourselves!

ROOT CHAKRA – (Base of spine/coccyx)

Oil	Cinnamon, Clove
Plant	Sage
Stone	Garnet, Hematite, Ruby
Color	Red
Element	Earth
Metal	Lead
Astrology	Capricorn
Angel	Michael
Positive Qualities	Mother being, nurturing, patience, manifesting your dreams, structure, encouragement, hope
Negative Qualities	Victim attitude, sadness, pessimism, and being too dependent on others can be victims of terrible circumstances, uprooted from life

AFFIRMATIONS/MANTRAS

Instead of a full-blown ceremonial ritual. Which is often unnecessary. It may be a good idea to say these affirmations/Mantras to yourself and see what aspect of your life they can help. Hence your focus on helping yourself and healing- not complaining.

- I Affirm my being before I can help others.
- I live life from the depths of my soul, longing to express myself.
- I know I am good and make choices based on what I know to be suitable.
- I stand for truth, honor, justice, and love.
- I live from my integrity.
- I am grateful for the challenges that have taught me who I truly am.
- I confirm my right to belong and be part of something greater than myself.
- GREAT SPIRIT WORDS AND HONOR CODE WORDS CAN BE SAID HERE.

YOGA POSES

I will do my best to suggest yoga poses for each chakra.
The root chakra uses a lot of legwork stretches, quadriceps, and hamstrings.

- Shallow frog pose/squat with hands in prayer
- Warrior 2
- Bridge hold
- Forward head-to-knee pose/hamstring stretch
- Balasana-Childs pose

SACRAL CHAKRA- (Between navel and pelvis)

Oil	Jasmine, neroli
Plant	Jasmine
Stone	Carnelian, Topaz, Tiger Eye, Onyx
element	Water
Color	Orange
Astrology	Scorpio
Metal	Tin
Angel	Metatron
Positive qualities	Well Being, sensuality, respect for the physical world, abundance, pleasure
Negative qualities	Martyring oneself, deprivation of self-pleasure, guilt

AFFIRMATIONS/MANTRAS

- I honor my body and treat myself respectfully
- I trust my feelings and give them room for expression
- I stimulate my immunity by knowing GOD lives in and through me
- I am well and surpass challenges/the norm
- Goodness, beauty, and joy resonate in my soul
- I deserve to enjoy and be enjoyed
- I heal any condition that affects me

YOGA POSES

- Goddess pose- High squat hands in prayer
- Reverse Warrior

- Padottasana- wide leg forward fold
- Seated forward bend
- Bridge with pelvic tilts

SOLAR PLEXUS CHAKRA- (located over the stomach)

Oil	Lemon, grapefruit, Juniper
Plant	Carnation
Stone	Topaz, Citrine, Amber
Color	yellow
Element	fire
Metal	Iron, Gold
Astrology	Aries, Leo
Angel	Uriel
Positive Qualities	Warrior, defined sense of self, inner strength, resilience, strong to meet challenges
Negative Qualities	Servant, seeking confirmation from others. Try to please others as they should please themselves

- I am worth my weight in gold
- I am worthy of the life I want.
- I am worthy of the best
- I know I am a powerful and wholesome force for good
- I am confident in my ability to make my life work
- I accept the power of being able to create love, health, and joy in my life
- I am worthy of love, kindness, and respect despite past actions

YOGA POSES

- Reverse plank- lie face up and straighten arms to hold the body up
- Bow pose-lie on the stomach-curve to reach the ankles
- Crescent pose- straight back leg lunge, reach to the sky
- Warrior pose- straight leg lunge, arms straight to sides as if pointing
- High lunge twist/prayer pose

HEART CHAKRA- (*middle of the chest*)

Oil	Rose, Carnation, Lily of the valley,
Plant	Foxglove, Rose Carnation, Lily
Stone	Rose quartz, Peridot
Element	Air
Color	Pink, Gold, Green
Astrology	Libra, Taurus
Metal	Copper, Gold
Angel	Raphael
Positive Qualities	Lover, love unconditionally, bring warmth and acceptance. Their love is inclusive. They share with everyone
Negative qualities	The actor, love is conditional. They have Judgement and criticism for anyone who does not fit their ideals

AFFIRMATIONS/MANTRAS

- I delight in sharing my joy
- I share from the depths of my being with those who accept
- I am love. I am at peace. I am light
- I choose the peace that surpasses understanding
- I desire to be united with all beings
- I am quiet and listen to my heart's song
- I look for the joy in myself and see it in all things

YOGA POSES

- Upward facing dog
- Fish pose- lie flat on the back, raise the heart to the sky with elbows bent straight under the shoulders
- Tree pose- stand tall with leg bent on the opposite knee, hands in prayer
- Camel pose- bend back to reach/hold ankles, chin to the sky
- Cobra pose- lie on the stomach, support the upper body on straight arms, turn the heart to the sky

THROAT CHAKRA - (center of the throat)

Oil	Chamomile, Gardenia
Plant	Gardenia
Stone	Turquoise, Blue agate, Aquamarine
Color	Turquoise
Element	The ethers that contain all
Metal	Mercury
Astrology	Gemini, Virgo
Angel	Gabriel
Positive Qualities	Communication, telling your truth, the strength of will, their words can be trusted
Negative Qualities	Suppression of expressiveness for fear and shame. Hiding feelings and not telling their truth.

AFFIRMATIONS/MANTRAS

- I communicate my truth
- I love to share my experiences and tell my story
- I listen to others' truth
- My word is my integrity. My word is my bond
- I appreciate silence
- I learn to listen to myself and trust my inner voice
- My communication comes from my deep center

YOGA POSES

- Head rolls
- Cat/Cow pose- on all fours, arch back, and reverse back
- Camel pose- backbend to reach ankles and hold
- Childs pose, crouch on legs, bend and reach forward
- Bridge pose- lie on your back with bent knees and arch back, push the upper body to the sky

BROW CHAKRA/THIRD EYE - (forehead center)

Oil	Camphor, Sweet Pea, Heliotrope
Plant	Almond blossom
Stone	Sapphire, Lapis Lazuli, Tanzanite
Color	Indigo Blue
Element	The Cosmos
Metal	Silver

Astrology	Sagittarius, Pisces
Angel	The Shekinah
Positive Qualities	Wisdom/ Elder, intuition, learned wisdom from life, balance physical and spiritual
Negative Qualities	Intellectual, only physical knowledge, dry thinking, analytical thought, no energy

AFFIRMATIONS/MANTRAS

- I think the very best of myself in all situations at all times
- I open myself to know my inner guidance and most profound wisdom
- I align my consciousness with the source of all life
- I release and forgive/learn from the past
- I open myself to new energy, people, places, and experiences
- I seek wisdom and guidance in all situations
- Communicating is vital to my well-being

YOGA POSES

- Kneeling and candle gazing
- Child's pose
- Wide-legged forward fold
- "aum" or sacred word

CROWN CHAKRA

Oil	Violet, Lavender, Lotus
Plant	Lotus Flower
Stone	Amethyst, Alexandrite, Clear Quartz
Color	Violet
Element	The Cosmos
Metal	Platinum
Astrology	Aquarius
Angel	The Christ Light
Positive Qualities	Master Teacher, the Divine force flows through you, deep consciousness, reflection
Negative Qualities	Egotists think their efforts alone carry them through life. They believe themselves separate from the greater whole of life

AFFIRMATIONS/MANTRAS

- God is in me and around me at all times
- I seek the highest truth and the most healing ways to live my life
- I honor and protect my Divine spirit
- I honor all people and all spiritual paths, all of which are Divine
- I accept who I am and honor the spirit within me
- I know my higher purpose is being fulfilled now
- My spirit is eternal. My love is beauty, harmony, peace, and joy

YOGA POSES

- Lotus pose/ cross-legged
- Rabbit, stand/kneel and lower the top of your head to touch the floor
- Corpse pose/ lie on back palms up/ still the mind
- Crocodile pose/ lie on your stomach, cross your arms under your forehead/ clear your mind.
- Cow face pose/ knees on top of each other, reach arms behind back and head

STRENGTH TRAINING FOR LOWER CHAKRAS

Root	Squats, Lunges, Leg Backlift, Leg side lift
Sacral	Bridge/pelvis tuck, knee/core pull, bicycle twist crunch
Solar Plexus	Alternate leg lift, Lying side leg lift, Legs pull-ups
Heart	Biceps curl, Crabwalk, pushups, Triceps kickback

There was a merchant in Bagdad who sent his servant to market to buy provisions, and in a little while, the servant came back, white and trembling, and said, "Master, just now, when I was in the marketplace, I was jolted by a woman in the crowd, and when I turned I saw it was Death that jostled me."

She looked at me and made a threatening gesture." Now, lend me your horse, and I will ride away from this city and avoid my fate. I will go to Samarra, and Death will not find me there." So the merchant lent him his horse, and the servant mounted it, and he dug his spurs in its flanks, and as fast as the horse could gallop, he went.

Then the merchant went down to the marketplace, and he saw me standing in the crowd, and he came to me and said, Why did you make a threatening gesture to my servant when you saw him this morning? That was not a threatening gesture, she said. It was only the start of the surprise. I was astonished to see him in Bagdad, for I had an appointment with him tonight in Samarra.

CONTINUING OUR JOURNEY

METHODS OF TOOL CHARGING

There is no one right method of tool charging. Yet the easiest to work with is the moon. On the other hand, some people work effortlessly with the Sun. If this is the case, do so.

For example:

The tools in question are magical tools such as The Wand, Athame, Sword, Censer, Pentacle, and Mirror, and even herbs or divinatory tools, anything to be used magically.

The best night to set out would be on the Full Moon.

Some tools may require Solar charging at dawn or midday, and the Solstices are used.

Some tools are solar only, such as certain tarots and stones. Yet many Draconic tools use both solar and lunar charges.

Certain Sabbats and times may have particular guidelines for ease if one wishes to use specific astrology. In addition, some herbs and candles used in certain spells may require waxing or waning moon charges, such as binding and success spell work tools.

A personal touch is required on many tools, such as Divinatory tools. This requires one to be in constant daily contact with them, such as sleeping with the Tool in question. The bond between you and the tool gets stronger as you do this more.

A person may wish to hold a circle specific to the charging process in other tools. This is done in addition to the lunar charging

This is a suggestion to many who may be wondering what to use as a Ritual, so I have penned this at request. Many will not wish to or find it necessary to follow this, which is alright. As this is a suggestion, the other rituals I will be writing in this book will be placed in the spell working period of the basic Sphere. If you have a better Rite that works for you, use it!! The point of the Ritual is to commune with the Deities and not have to follow any stringent rules. You should be comfortable, and it is necessary to have your heart in the right place. That is what is important!!

THE RITUAL ITSELF EXPLANATIONS...

(work with as you see fit)
Priest/ess states:
All who enter this Sphere do so with Universal order and chaos in their hearts, minds, and souls.

At the entry, all form a line of waiting in order of work, with their astral candles, and then are welcomed by the Priestess. Upon entry, each one is kissed and smudged with sage or other herbs.

The circle is drawn out, or the Maiden of Sphere escorts members to their space.

The energy flow is thus begun, and others circle in the corresponding direction.

Music, bells, or the playing of sacred instruments herald the beginning of Sphere and promote energy flow.

Once all are entered, create space by palm circling to begin the flow through all. Chanting or singing with the leader 3x is a standard round.

We then return to the altar, and those chosen to consecrate the physical elements do so.

Quarters can be called using the guided words or your own, as can consecrations.

At the very first, those call all the Quarters. The Quarters need to be present at the consecration of the Elements. These can be done at the same time or in turn. It is up to those chosen to decide. A chant, little song, or playing is done if they are done singularly.

The priest-ess goes to the element, welcoming with the Athame and charging behind and with the quarter caller.

First, the consecration of Earth and water is done, and the sphere circle is completed. After the Altar candle is circled with. Then Air and Fire are consecrated together. Consecration strengthens the elemental bond of protection, and recasting the circle reinforces the strength.

The energy must flow at a relaxed pace; flowing through one's hands and tools to create sigils attracts specific deities. For example, the Priest-ess circles with the Altar Candle, the Salt, and Water or Earth and Water are seen as Feminine spirits and are symbols of the Mother Goddess. Air and Fire are seen as Masculine spirits and are symbols of the Father God. However, Earth and Air do sometimes play back and forth.

North is the Spirit direction of Earth. It is symbolized as a light green candle in the waxing moon phase -NF or a black candle in the waning moon phase- FD.

(New to full moon NF)
(Full to Dark moon FD)

'Silence and resonance' are meditated upon as mysteries of the psychological virtues of Earth.

East is the spiritual direction of Air and is seen as white candle NF or yellow candle FD, and its psychological virtues for meditation are to 'wonder and know.'

South is Fire's spiritual direction, symbolized as an orange candle NF or dark red candle FD.

Its psychological virtues for meditation are to 'surrender and will.'

West is the spiritual direction of the element of water. West is symbolized as light blue NF or dark blue FD. The psychological virtues to meditate upon are 'acceptance and daring.'

Quarters are being called for those who are not busy; these can create and keep the energy flowing through spiraling, dancing, and song. Then, when all is complete, make another palm circle and reaffirm the power of the sphere.

During the invocation of Deities-energies, all can participate, Meditate on seeing or bringing the God/ess into you or any deity one may feel comfortable with.

When energy is at its peak, the Priest/ess will make an invoking spiral.

Great Spirit words and Unification are done here as well.

THE CHARGE- Deities have their charges; use them if you have appropriate words.

WAND- creates and sends energy forces; it is more potent if made by your hand. Air is its element.

STAFF- This is a giant wand representing honor and authority. It is a symbol of discipline after many years. The Staff/Wand is a symbol of the element of air.

SWORD- is a vessel of Dragon Power, and it is better if your hand makes some part. The Sword is a symbol of fire and the South. It is a very large Athame.

These two can cut, create in all forms, and send energy mainly to Draconic beings; these also never touch blood.

ATHAME- a small sword can only cut, send energy, or carve in the circle. Its elemental direction is South. The Athame also never touches blood.

DRAGON IMAGE- A personal vessel made by your hand and the home of your Dragon, and many Draconic beings can work through it. ALL elements are present in this.

HERALDING STAFF- Earth-air, The Heralding staff is used on Sabbats to Herald, a Grand celebration to the Deities. It is sacred to the East, and Air.

CAULDRON- Fire, Earth, or water. If placed in the West, this can be used for water scrying or water spells. If set in the South for fire spells and scrying. North – well, the metal-iron makes this an earthly tool.

MIRROR- It is an inter-dimensional doorway and is used for Draconic spells.

BLACK MIRROR- This is hand-made and attuned to you. It is used as a mental scrying piece and may talk to you. The Black Mirror can be used in dark mysteries and waning-dark moon work.

SMUDGE- This cleanses energy and or mundane negativity as you enter the circle.

STONES- These attract desired energy and specific Dragons or Deities and can be used in spells. These can be placed in a bowl on the altar, around the Altar candle, At the rim, or around the circle. These magnify the power within and represent the Earth.

CRYSTAL BALLS- Clear quartz projects NF energy, and obsidian projects FD energy. Sabbats can rarely be held on the day or time necessary, so place your ball of choice outside to collect the energy of the day and time. When brought into the circle you will release the desired power.

GREAT SPIRIT WORDS- The Great Spirit Words were written to fit many mystical paths. We believe all deities are like personality traits of the one great Transcendent Spirit. This is unisexual-or androgynous, unfathomable, and perhaps familiar; it is meant to be! **THERE IS NO ONE TRUE PATH FOR ALL PEOPLE.** We look to find mystical teaching in all things **DRACONIS SEEKS TO WELCOME ALL AND ALL IS ONE!**

DEDICATION- After a time, which can be seen by both priest/ess. Or one may choose to dedicate themselves to the universe. The commitment states your allegiance to the Dragon, Deities, Energies, and Spirits.... Much discipline in all forms is required, looked at, and tested for in about three to six mos. And they are repeated about every year.

SYMBOLIC GREAT RITE- UNIFICATION

Since Draconis uses symbols, the Symbolic Great Rite is done with Priest/ess, with the Priestess holding a chalice of red wine representing the Lady. Next, the Priest holds and plunges slowly into the red wine, the Athame, with representative Sacred words. Then all form pentacles on the head, heart, and abdomen of another until all participants are blessed. Then each takes a sip of the wine honoring the Blessed union.

Statement of intent is made to Deity-s depending on the situation

WORKING PERIOD - This is used for any spellwork of sorts or scrying. Writing is done and either buried with libations or burned. The Palm circle binds energy and brings all members to act together once again. If necessary, we will ground by touching the earth first and then make a circle to reconnect as a community.

CAKES AND ALE/LIBATION-Priest/ess first circles with food and drink.3x round toast to Deities we wish to thank and why

GOOD JOURNEY-Done through all elements in reverse of casting. Last grounding circle to close sphere.

A Sphere is never-ending, and the power cuts through the Earth and Sky. A Sphere is also very sacred and a time outside of time for all who wish to reach an authentic Mystical experience. Remember, a Totem and a Spiritual Path and Deity(S) choose you!!

DRACONIS SPHERE- WEEKLY RITE

This is the basic Draconic circle upon which all other rituals can be patterned, and spell workings can be inserted into.

Priest/ess Casts saying-

I create this Sphere of power and dedicate it to the Ancient ones. Here they manifest and bless their children.

All enter and make a palm circle song leader leads a chant

This is a time that is not a time, in a place that is not a place. So we welcome all into the Sacred circle as we stand at the threshold between the worlds before the veil of mysteries. May the Ancient ones help and protect us on our magical journey!

North lights the candle and greets the element.

May this Sacred space be created by the earth's womb and the powers of the North, guard this circle, and give your aid to this rite

Earth sets salt on SPIRAL and charge.

Great Mother, bless this spirit of the earth to your service. May we always remember that earth is lifegiving!

Circle area with charged earth. Place charged earth on the north edge of the altar, or if outside, next to the earth candle. All say -

Great Mother, we give you honor

East- light the candle and greet

Great Father, Bless this spirit of air to your service. May we always listen to the spirit winds on which travel the voices of the ancient ones so that we may understand them well, guard this circle and give your aid to this rite!

Circle the area with charged incense and lightly blow incense smoke around and inside the perimeter. Place charged incense on the north edge of the altar, or if outside, next to the air candle

Great father, we give you honor!

South- light the candle and greet

May this sacred space be warmed by the fires of the south. Guard this circle and give your aid to this rite!

Set fire candle on Spiral, charge saying,

Great Father, bless this spirit of fire to your service. May the sacred flame add warmth to our lives.

Circle area with charged fire. Place charged fire on the south edge of the altar, or if outside, in the south.

May this sacred space be born from the waters of the west. Guard this circle and give your aid to this rite!

Set water on the spiral on the altar and charge by saying

Great Mother, Bless this spirit of water to your service. May we always remember the cauldron waters of rebirth!

Circle the area with charged water. Lightly spritz the perimeter and circle with sacred water. Place charged water on the west edge of the altar. Or if outside, next to the water candle at the Sphere's edge. All say-

Great Mother, we give you honor!

Priest-ess-Center lights Altar candle and Greet, Invoking of ENERGIES-DEITIES, etc. Spirit flame is lit. The spirit Flame container is a small iron container/cauldron filled with Everclear or Bacardi 151, then lit! saying

May all within the Sacred Sphere gain the understanding and wisdom of spirit, encompassing our universes known and unknown. Guard this Sphere and all within, bringing forth knowledge, wisdom, and understanding of order and chaos to be felt and known. Give your aid to this rite!

Let energy flow and sing or chant priest/ess, then states

We consecrate this place of the rite with earth, water, smoke, and firelight. This Sphere is bound with power all around. Between the worlds, we stand with protection at hand.

All participants write their wishes/spell works. Depending on the moon, these are either buried or burned. Light the Spirit flame; then all say the

Great Spirit Words

Found in the <u>Sacred Words</u> section

By the power of the Ancient ones, I bind all energy into this working for the good of all! So mote it be! We invite you to join our celebration!

Celebrants, in turn, honor deities of choice and libate!

Three times round toast with all is made. Thanks to the elements is done in reverse.

All touch the ground and connect to the earth. Elemental participants are in charge of closing their elements before releasing the circle

Depart in peace, O powers of West and Water. We give thanks to you for your aid in this rite!

Each elemental person repeats for -fire and south, air and incense, north and earth!
Return to altar

To all beings of the visible and invisible. We give thanks to you for your aid in this rite! Merry meet, merry part, and merry meet again!

Priest-ess walks widdershins, holding Athame, toward the outside perimeter of the circle and says.

The Sphere is open yet not broken forever it remains a Sphere. Around and through us flows its magic always!

POLARITY/SOLAR/LUNAR/WYRD

These energies are distinct, and most prefer to work primarily with one another. The two can be performed synonymously. After that, it is up to the mage. Lunar energy is predominantly feminine, has a negative polarity, and begins each Celtic day, certain Sabbats, and seasons. Solar energy is primarily masculine, has a positive polarity, is linear, and begins the Nordic/Roman days. Some Sabbats and seasons. The three aspects of Draconis deal with all of these.

Asa- is solar/masculine- straightforward

Vana- is Lunar/feminine, mysterious

Wyrd- utilizes both lunar and solar, is balancing

Sphere Draconis utilizes all. The Solar, Lunar, and Wyrd

Each person may work better with one form than the other, Solar-Lunar-Wyrd. This is a normal thing.
There are also tools specific to the various energies. As one practices and becomes more in tune with these energies, they will

learn, and their understanding will grow. The means one chooses to use are many. Examples would be, Runes, Tarot, pendulums, etc. Yet, solar AND lunar energies are needed to cleanse and charge any tool completely.

To fully understand universal energies, they must be felt/experienced. Hence I say practice is best for all. It is best to utilize mental quiet and listening. Meditate on your surroundings, physical and vibrational. This will happen to you! Deities of all sorts will be attracted to and want to work with you! Whether you see them as Dragons, Fey, plant or animal totems, etc.

SPELL WORK VS. TRANSFORMATION

Almost anyone can follow a simple set of instructions as in a recipe. Yet, the whys and wherefores of pursuing a specific direction need to be explained. So a person can dissect what needs to be done and if a spell change is necessary.

Thus is the GREAT importance of extended silence and listening, not just to each other but also to other unphysical beings. Questions always need to be asked, for a spell or folk magic does not explain why things are such a way—bringing about little change unless this is understood.

The practitioner's knowledge of such details in a spell is essential for success.

Education in Self Transformation is what this book is about

Everyone is essential for learning from and within each other once one learns to quiet oneself and listen within and out, sharing with others as needed.

The answers come from within ourselves and the spirits around us, and we are thus ready.

Listening from within is a great achievement, and all magic, as one will learn, is correct in some form, and their path is waiting for them. If a path is wrong for a person, they do not need to follow it but learn from the experience.

BASIC ENERGY

Energy is a result of vibration. It is what gives us the feeling to act. A person's energy is also magnetic and attracts like energies. Energy is talked about by many about as strong or weak. Energy can be explained as firmness in control one has over their physical presence. A wishy-washy person, more than likely, has weak energy.

A person's energy may not be attractive to another because it may vibrate differently.

However, please beware of the false people who can manipulate energy as they attract weaker beings who do not know what may happen. These dishonest beings are like the liars we detest covering for dishonorable actions in the future. Hoping this will make others find them to be innocent of harm. Beware of these beings!

Back on the topic is an example of low-frequency beings who may be misunderstood as Dark or "Death" spirits/entities. They are not evil but alien. Their likes and feelings may be different from many others. The question is, "do these spirits harm life for no reason?"

This is the first of many reasons a covener must be 18, as the law of the land states.

Free will is an essential factor for all parties involved.

In old times ritual sex had no specifics around the convention. This was a reason for years of bloodshed begun by other religions and led to persecutions; thus, a sacred circle was created.

Ritual sex is an act of creation of all life from the Lord & Lady.

Ritual sex is a method of raising magical energy. Magical energy is understood in the representation of the Lady & Lord honoring each other and taking pleasure in each other.

The polarity of males and Females is energetically produced and felt by all.

The Symbolic Great Rite was added in time, using the red wine and athame; yes, the actual ceremony raises the energy, yet so does the symbolic; the participants focus all creative energy.

Many words must have their differences explained for them to be understood.

UNDERSTANDING VIBRATIONAL ENERGY

The American Heritage Dictionary defines it as id oscillation of a particle, particles, or elastic solid or surface, back and forth across a central position.

I will use this and its scientific definition. When Vibration is used, we refer to a person's physical and etheric cells. These vibrations can be felt by many despite their skills. Therefore, altering a vibrational frequency is beneficial for attracting- repelling others.

Life forms will flock around anything with a vibrational frequency with which they resonate. Life forms will avoid anything with a vibrational frequency they do not like. This is an effective way to alter energy.

YEARLY SABBATS

Each sabbat is different in its mythology as other world areas are its origin. This is a regular thing. For instance, the Winter Solstice is Celtic, and Yule is Norse and celebrated differently in certain lands. Many world areas have a significant celebration around a critical holy day. The mythology may be different. Still, again this proves universal psychology—the communication of stories as people traveled.

Making the Sabbats match and have rhyme and reason is not reasonable, for the different traditions celebrate all of them differently- the Sabbats should be more original. What is important is listening and feeling the Earth's rhythm and cycles and putting those into the ritual. Then you are indeed in tune with the land. Examples are:

Imbolc- celebrates the upcoming warm season and the growth of the earth to come
Ostara- marks the balance and visible change within the world and our lives.
Beltane- the light veil lifted to commune with spirits and celebrated sensually, magically, and physically.
Litha- celebrating the apex of the sun and the coming of the Waning sun.

Llughnasadh- the first harvest and celebrating the life of lord Lugh.
Mabon- celebrating the balance in our lives and the Earth again and thanks and harvesting.'
Samhain- the dark, mysterious veil lifting for ancestor celebrating. There is much more, but one's intuition answers best as these Holy days are personally experienced.

SAMHAIN

Many people go overboard with Samhain, and I feel you would be okay with the basics since there is so much! But, unfortunately, people act as though this is the only day to be celebrated!

Samhain is the beginning of the year in Celtic lands, a lunar celebration. It begins at sundown the night before, on October 31eve. The day is November 1.

Samhain is the 3rd and final harvest festival. Imbolc and Beltane its predecessors. Maiden Mother and Crone.

All foods must be harvested by Samhain this time, or they will be cursed and unusable, so the legend goes.

Samhain is the festival sacred to Dark Deities, the Morrighan, Hecate, and the God's dark aspect in his many Death forms. This is a time of crows' communication with universal magical realms—a time of learning universal laws corresponding to death.

Samhain is so close to death-rebirth deities as the dark half of the year. This is the perfect time to aid spirits in crossing the veil and embracing and conquering fears. All dark shadow work is completed on his time.

SAMHAIN RITE

This could be done alone or inserted in the spell-working portion of Sphere!

The altar is prepared with mini candleholders three black, one white, two gold, one red, and one orange candle. Corn dolls, or any figures made from the husks of corn. Decorated with corn silks, they are used in the ritual, as well as a staghorn.

A separate Ancestor altar is designated for those we wish to remember, using pictures, flowers, stones, etc.

Priestess holds corn doll aloft

I light three candles for the Great Ladies of three aspects.

Light white candle

Glorious Maiden who symbolizes youth and new beginnings

light red candle

Great Mother Goddess of magic, honor, balance, and knowledge

Light black candle

Dark Crone, Goddess of the night, eternal life, death, and rebirth, Lady of Shadows, the giver of light and wisdom, paradoxically

The priest holds antler aloft

Three candles I light for the Great Father of many faces

yellow light candle

We honor the Bright Lord of success and fruition

green candle lit

Lord of the woodlands, fertility, and growth.

black candle lit

Dark Lord of the Underworld, of protection, rest, and giver of life

Pries/tess lights candle in the west

The West is the Land of the Dead; this night is the Feast of the Dead. The night of the Wheel turning, another cycle to be

completed and start anew. The gates between all worlds are open this night and shall pass through the thin veil.

>Priest/ess says, and all repeat

This is Ancestor night, the strongest for communication with those gone into the Summerland; listen to ancient wisdom all!! The veil is lifted; let those dear ones who have gone before return on this night to make merry with us, for they are welcomed into this space.

>Priest/ess raises arms and says

O thou Divine giver of peace and rest, we shall enter thy realms unafraid and gladly, for we know that Death is an aspect of life that takes us into another realm and teaches us to grow!
May we meet, learn, and remember

>All move Widdershins around the altar and move back to regular positions, saying

The Wheeling year has turned again, and the final Harvest has come this year. We have sown many seeds. Let the good be harvested and cast aside those that would harm!

>All take a few moments and meditate on the past year speaking aloud, so if they wish, when all are done, say;

Give us explicit knowledge, Ancient ones, hear our desires, guide and protect us. Please lead us to greater understanding, wisdom, and fulfillment.

>All write desires or banishings, state them silently, and then bury or burn them
>After many libations to the dead, all (or continue with crossing rites) drink from the same chalice, saying

Merry do we meet, merry shall we part, and merry shall we meet again

Everyone processes to the Ancestor Altar, a separate altar for the belongings of those Dead we honor on this night.
Place special flowers-gifts and use Copal, Myrrh, and Dragons Blood incense
Priest-ess Washes circle members hands with water and spritz with these words

I am washing the grief and unhappiness away from your spirit. May it cleanse your whole being as the water cleanses your hands and you are sprinkled with this Sacred water

At the same time, Priest-ess instructs the member to state the deceased person to be honored, Name, job, talent, background, love, faith, etc.
Statement of intent is said -decided on earlier
Beckon the Dead to enter and be welcome with reading, then meditation

People state what the Summerland in passing is to them

3 min beat and silence
Priest/ess- goes to the gate, and all lift veil to open, bid farewell, and love

Memories live on and never die; hence you will always be with us, even crossed over! So farewell and good journey, dear ones! Great Guardians----are ready to join you now!

Close gate
Reconnect with the Earth and each other
Song or chant if you choose

<u>*SOLSTICE/YULE/CHRISTMAS*</u>

When you choose a pantheon or tradition that seems right to you, you decide what you resonate with or respond to on a spiritual level. The separate Deities in these many pantheons help us bring certain aspects of ourselves out. These details exist in many traditions worldwide, from Christmas to Yule to Solstice.

Everyone shares specific inherent Human Rights simply because they are part of the human race. Of course, people are very different; they come in two main genders: different sizes, colors, and shapes; many races; differing sexual orientations; and different degrees of ability. In addition, they follow many Religious and economic systems, speak many languages, and follow many different cultures. But there is a growing consensus that all people are equal in importance. All should enjoy fundamental Human rights without having beliefs forced upon them, as all choose. The Universal **Declaration of Human Rights** makes this very clear.

Nothing was questioned as evil. Evil is part of a duality of separateness among the Celts; many did not care for it. All of the universes had "good and evil," positive and negative, for that is how things are. The Celts looked at this big picture called the Earth-Universe and understood that people must leave everything be, for if it was in balance and harmony with all, then why fix it?

The middle of winter has long been a time of celebration worldwide. Centuries before the man's arrival called Jesus, early Europeans celebrated light and birth on winter's darkest days. Many peoples rejoiced during the **Winter Solstice** when the worst of the winter was behind them, and they could look forward to longer days and extended hours of sunlight. This period is around December 21 and celebrates the Birth of light, the Sun's return, warmth, and the welcoming warmth the Light God has to bring. Hence Jesus' birth was the best story used by Christians to explain the return of light to the world.

From December 21, the Winter Solstice, the Norse celebrated Yule through January in Scandinavia. In recognition of the sun's return, fathers and sons would bring home large logs, called Yule Logs, a symbol of the Solstice and Yuletide.

In Germany, people honored the Pagan God *Odin* during the mid-winter holiday. However, many believed he made nocturnal flights through the sky called Odin's Wild Hunt. Germans were in awe of Odin, who rides his famous Sleipnir Horses throughout the skies. Mother Berchta accompanies him on Skeggi, a 15-foot-tall Goat.

Pope Julius the First chose December Twenty-fifth as the Christian celebration. It is commonly believed that the Church decided to adopt and absorb the traditions of many Pagan festivals. In Rome, where winters were not as harsh as those in the far north, **Saturnalia** was celebrated—a holiday in honor of Saturn, the God of agriculture. Also, around the winter solstice, Romans observed **Juvenalia,** a feast honoring Rome's children. Finally, the upper-class members often celebrated Mithra, the God of the unconquerable sun, on December 25.

There are many different symbols associated with the many varying traditions of winter, and I have listed a few with their basic meanings:

OAK

It is associated with light and the Light God. These trees attract lightning. The magic within these is one of the most acceptable fertility symbols. They also have phallic symbols of the acorn.

HOLLY

Associated with the dark half of the year, the Dark God, immortality, and a dark, mysterious Elf king on the dark, mysterious side. The Holly berries are seen as drops of blood, giving life, and the bushes are said to keep away damaging spells. The Holly King is the Green man in another guise. Holly is a symbol of rebirth.

IVY

being an evergreen plant represents eternity, fidelity, and strong affectionate attachment, such as wedded love and friendship. The Ivy plant is also vigorous and can grow in the most challenging environment.

Another association of Ivy as an evergreen is perennial life and immortality. It may also represent dependence and attachment, which can be seen in how it climbs trees and buildings to get sunlight. The Ivy leaf also represents the phallic, depicting the male trinity, but it can also be a female symbol denoting a force in need of protection. Conversely, its harmful, poison feature can often cause it to be mistaken for ingratitude.

POINSETTIAS

An old Mexican myth says a boy wanted to give the Christ child a gift but was poor and couldn't buy anything, and the divine intervened and the Poinsettia sprang up at the boys' feet.

REINDEER

Symbolic of the stags that drew the Norse gift-giving goddess Mother Berctha. Also symbolic of Odin's Sleipnir.

MISTLETOE

It symbolizes the semen of God and was used to bring fertility and abundance.

ANGELS

There are many types, the love and knowledge angels of the Cherubim, The singing and healing in all forms, Archangels, Seraphim, Thrones - Divine
    Messengers, Principalities- Angels ruling over the powers in the flesh and mind, and over the management race, and Virtues- angels of morals.
    Many traditions share many parallels a person can see, but how the nice myth of Santa Claus and his reindeer came about and the light child's birth. So many of the "Nice" stories we tell our children have a "Truth," whether in myth or basic symbology, over many ages.

YULE LOG INSTRUCTIONS

    Many people have said creating a Yule log MUST follow many rules. No!! Just a few! It is good to have all contradictions represented here, as this symbolizes polarities. Oak and Holly- represent the dark and light polarities. Plus, the female and male.
    The candles used are mainly red, green, yellow, and blue, but variations can easily be. The log can be either Oak or an Evergreen wood such as Cedar. They both represent new life- Oak is a must in

some form, but that is ONLY BECAUSE Oak was the most common tree in Europe, and Yule logs came from the Anglo-Saxon way of life.

The many decorations are personal, and I have left a list of totems to understand and decide what they represent. A Yule Log is unique to the person or group and should be a physical representation of that. I decorate my log with four holes to hold four candles at the top. Spots for a brown or black candle, a yellow candle, a red candle, and a green candle are drilled into it. I decorate it with Oak leaves, Holly leaves, and Mistletoe leaves. I also use colored ribbons to decorate it.

YULE/SOLSTICE/CHRISTMAS RITE

Insert into spell working section of Sphere

The Priest and Priestess don Christmastide cloaks. The Priest is wearing a dark cloak,
Underneath his Christmastide cloak is a lighter
Priestess lights red and green candles saying

This is the Winter Solstice, the longest night of the year. Darkness reigns triumphant yet gives way and changes into light.

The candles on the Yule log are lit one red, one green, one brown/black, and one yellow
All repeat

All is cold, and I await the coming of the dawn. As the sun rises, the triple Goddess once more gives birth to the Divine child. In silence and wonder, we stand before Eternal Life and rebirth, knowing that one day we must pass through and be reborn.

Light a standing lone Black candle on the altar surrounding the log, Priestess says

This candle will draw to Earth all the balance of the Universe

Light a standing lone Gold candle on the altar surrounding the log as the Priest says

This candle will send light into the world to bring bounty, balance, and peace. This will bring light to all, to renew the light once again!

The Priest says, and all repeat

The velvet darkness transforms to everlasting light, ablaze with glory! I was reborn to start again on the perennial cycle of lively adventure! Through death and birth, we experience life everlasting.
Most Ancient Ones, we awaken in us the power of thy will; kindle within me thy eternal flame! Split the darkness asunder and illuminate the earth both within and without! Finally, complete the ending so we may begin a new spiral!

The Priest changes coak from the dark cloak to the Lighter mantle underneath. Each person discusses the differing aspects of Yule/Solstice and what the growing sun and light mean to them. Spiral dancing and continual chanting are good to raise energy or circle sun-wise chanting.

As the new is born, so the old shall die and be reborn!
Sing of choice or story tell.

IMBOLC

Imbolc is traditionally held on Feb. 1, and after the cold harshness of winter, this Sabbat celebrates the Goddess welcoming the youthful Sun God returning to her in spring. This Sabbat is also called Oimelc, when ewes began lactating, which was a sign that winter was ending. This Sabbat was sacred to the Goddesses Brigit, Bloddeuwedd, and Venus. Many candles and fires were lit at this time, for the ancients thought it was good to lure back the sun.
The Sun Wheel or Brigit cross is a symbol for Imbolc.
Hearts are associated with Imbolc, for there was an ancient Druidic practice of divining from the heart removed from a living white bull.

Also, a traditional time to collect stones, and rocks, thought by the Druids and other mages to have a life of their own, divining would be done with stones.

Use this time to prepare for the new spring by consecrating your soil and seeds of a plant to start to grow in the next month. The Imbolc rite can also be done in combination with the Valentines Rite if one chooses

I love making fey wine, and it is delicious! One Quart of goat's milk. Mix in 1/4C Honey, a pinch of vanilla, cinnamon, and or cloves. To honor the Ewes lactating!

IMBOLC RITE

Also inserted in the spell working section of Sphere

The Imbolc rite should be prepared with a white altar cloth, a white candle, a very light green candle, potting soil, a Peridot or greenstone, a flowerpot, white flower seeds, and spring water. Celebratory Faery Imbolc wine is made with goats' milk and 1- 3 tbs honey to taste. This honors honor the fey for this rite. Nothing is to be planted, only prepared to grow and consecrate on Ostara.

Priest-ess says these or other guiding words

"Mother Earth stirs from her long slumber. The fields and forests hear her whisper them awake. The creatures of her realms answer her summons; everything waits in anticipation for spring. I charge these candles with Her power to draw all the knowledge needed for our sovereignty into this magic place."

Light the white candle on the East side of the flowerpot and the green candle on the west side of the flower pot.
The Priestess holds the Faery wine over the incense, saying

I call into this sacred space the Great Mothers of fertility.

The Priest places Athame blade into milk, saying

I draw into this sacred space the energy of the Lord who shares creation eternal

All say

0The waters of life shall bring protection, health, and fertility for all. Sun and Earth infuse us from within as we absorb the waters of everlasting creation.

All drinks from chalice beginning in the
south-The Priest/ess says:

This is the festival of the Maiden, who shares with all the breath of life. This is a time of waxing light and receding darkness. This is a season of purification and renewal of life.

Earth quarter person begins to put soil in pot saying

I salute the glorious Maiden preparer of new life out of the darkness. So may this Earth bring about bounty and life anew as our Glorious Maiden spreads her blessings over the land.

Air quarter charges stone to be later placed in soil for growth.

O great Lord and Lady, make our lives fertile with good health, prosperity, and magic, as the winds of life bring forth new growth within all things upon this Earth.

Fire quarter says, charging seeds for later use

Behold the Lord of the forests caresses the dreaming Earth. As there is a renewal in all plants and animals, so shall there be renewal in our lives.

Water quarter charges pure water for plant saying

Behold these waters of life that bring forth new growth. All life comes from a source, which needs a partner to create,

earth-water, fire-air, and Goddess-God. May these waters aid in creating a new life for all.

A drop of milk from the Fey Wine is added to the soil, and when potting is done.

May this sacred life nurture health, prosperity, and success. We thank you, Maiden and Lord, for your blessings. Merry shall we meet merry shall we part, and merry shall we meet again.

Keep the soil pot in a safe place 2-3 days before the Equinox, soak seeds in the water, and refrigerate.

OSTARA

The celebration we know as Ostara/Spring Equinox was celebrated long before the Christian Easter, which takes place on the first Sunday AFTER the first Full Moon AFTER the Spring Equinox. At the Equinoxes, night and day are of equal length worldwide. Therefore, this is the day most people recognize Springtime and the rebirth of new life.

The Maiden Goddess gives birth to the power of the Sun. The Spring Equinox is the official day many recognize as the beginning of Spring. Springtime is the season of rebirth. The Maiden Goddess becomes a Mother giving birth to the Sun God's power.

Easter(Ostara) is a festival of the spring Goddess Eostre. She is a Northern Teutonic variation of Ostara, Ishtar, and Isis. She is a Goddess of fertility and a personification of the East, Morning, and Spring. Many also depict her holding an egg in her hand.

That egg she holds symbolizes newborn life, creation and rebirth, split open by the heat of the Sun God. The color scarlet or red is life's color. There is a rabbit that hops playfully around her. This rabbit is associated with what we know as the Easter Bunny, Her totem animal.

The Full Moon after the Spring Equinox is meant to illustrate the pregnant phase of Eostre, the fertile season. The welsh Blodeuwedd is another Goddess of Earth's renewal. She is a Faery Queen and giver of life. All herald the arrival of spring.

The Easter Lily is a traditional Easter flower. The plant Totem of Eostre is the floral emblem/totemic flower of the Goddess Juno in her virgin aspect, and Eostre as well as Lilith, who gave her name to the Lily. Lilith is also the (dark aspect) of Bodeuwedd and Eostre. The Lily is the symbol of purity, fertility, and life anew! The egg (world egg) symbolizes rebirth and energy in becoming and growth! The color silver represents the Moon, gold or yellow. The Sun and red, the blood of life!

SPRING EQUINOX/ OSTARA RITE

Inserted in the spell working section of sphere

The altar cloth is usually light green; seeds and soil blessed at Imbolc are needed. Candles of white, black, yellow, lt. green, pink, and red are required as well. Make hardboiled painted eggs and have some rabbit fur; a live rabbit is excellent! Decorate the altar with flowers if you have them.
White and black candles are already lit.
Priest/ess says, and all repeat.

I welcome to this sacred space the Goddess Ostara! I ask with the flickering of this flame that she joins this Magic circle

Women repeat after the anointed green candle is lit

O lovely faery Queen Blodeuwedd, Ostara, and Cernunnos be with us! Bring the delights of spring, the power of fertility, and the joy of beauty

The Priest/ess holds a painted egg to the sky, and all repeat

Goddess Ostara, bring your life energy to this world and renew in nature, the animals, and the land again. Renew life in all beings to end destruction!

The Priest/ess says, and all men repeat

O mighty lovely Blodeuwedd cast the spell of beauty, health, and happiness to all here on Earth.

The Priest/ess then lights an anointed Yellow candle

All hail and welcome! Hear the call of the Faery Queen Blodeuwedd and the Goddess Ostara. This is a time of happiness as we see the growth of Flora.

Earth quarter charges soil with Athame and intentions. The soil is passed through incense, and then the Fire Quarter sets the seeds, and all say together

Behold the Lord of the forests caresses the Earth. As there is renewal in all plants and animals, so shall there be renewal in our lives!

Earth quarter then plants seeds, and water is charged, saying;

Behold these Waters of life that bring forth new growth. May these waters aid in creating a new life for all.

Then seeds are watered. Hold the rabbit or the rabbit fur in your hands aloft. Charge it and ask Ostara to bless it with her magic. Raise the item overhead;

We honor the God of Light and the Goddess of beauty and life! We send this magic to the winds of change and the universe itself.

Touch the Earth

BELTANE

Beltuinn or Bealtaine is a Gaelic word that means the whole month of May. So May Day is the first day, and Walpurgisnacht is May eve, about April 30. Walpurga is the Christian variation of the Teutonic Earth mother, Walburg. Others are Cerridwen. Cernunnos or Llugh are the male deities of this time. Lady Day, Rudemas, and Cyntefyn are other names for that period.

As the Celtic day begins the night before, the celebrations begin. Beltane is the light half of Samhain, which is dark and heralds the Celtic New Year,

Beltane is either experienced or timed at the Full moon in Taurus or May 1.

This period heralds the light half of the year. Beltane is a day that also heralds the arrival of the Tuatha de Dannan to the shores of Erin.

Beltane is a time of the immense Sun, as Samhain is a time of the little Sun. These are the two times when the veils between the planes-worlds are the absolute thinnest of all days.

May is a time of fertility and new beginnings, a great time of the lady and the lord, and is hugely Fey-oriented, for one can work with them more easily.

On this eve, the Celts would build fires of nine Sacred kinds of wood and, with the magical properties of the Holy fire, jump over the flames, run between them if there were two fires, and drive herds between them for protection.

Bel is a Celtic god known as the "Bright, Shining one" with solar-like qualities. He is the British equivalent of the Gallic Cernunnos or Lugh. Beltane is a time of the melding of the forces between males and females. The Oak tree symbolizes the God of the Waxing year, as Hawthorne symbolizes the Goddess of the waxing year.

Hawthorne, in tradition, is picked only once a year. The Blackthorn or Sloe tree is also sacred to the Goddess but in her crone aspect.

The sacrifice and rebirth at Beltane symbolize balance as the Earth's fertility is said to take place. But, again, the period is Lunar, mainly at the Full moon's peak, and each person will experience this differently.

A concentration of Light Fey, Senchus- master- high formal Deities are used and welcomed from around the Universe. Many people will work with much energy differently, and these energies communicate with each person.

A sample Beltane rite, this is the ritual of Bealtaine.

BELTANE RITE

Insert in the Spellworking part of the ritual. You can also do this in unison with the Faery Rite in the Personal Rituals section

Prepare an Altar with flowers, leaves, and bouquets for libations and gifts. As we did in Ostara, many plants need to be planted and fertilized at this time. You may choose as you will, but Honeysuckle and Butterfly Bush are the examples I'll use. My advice- refer to the Western Garden book for plants to use! Royal blue, green, orange, and rose mini candles, and any decoration or statuary you may find appropriate., and Beltane-type incense (in the recipes section). Cast a colossal circle to encompass all frivolity and Maypole! Have Maypole ready for fertility dance with ribbons.

All say:

We Celebrate the Bealtaine Period of Cetsamhain, returning life and fertility to the world.

If possible, the ritual will be done with a bird out in the circle area, a spider, or any Fey creature. Circle with votives, and in between will be small glasses of whiskey or scotch. Libations will be sung or stated in rhyme, and green apples and iced tea; for all the wicked stepmothers and good fairies. If you can get a Copper cauldron, use it! Iron is not a danger at all. That is FALSE- thank you, Shakespeare!!! This Rite can be done at any phase of the moon and most deities. This Rite can be done in unison or a combination of the Spider/ Norn Rite as the Norns, as they are the eldest Faeries in the world!

Light Green mini candle

We celebrate the growing year.

Light orange candle

We celebrate the coming warmth.

Light royal blue candle

We Give honor to the royal God in all his forms.

Light rose mini candle:

We give honor to the Royal Goddess in all her forms

> At the beginning of Sphere, each participant carries each treasure. A spear, sword, stone, and cauldron
>
> Participant in North
>
> Plant the bush of choice, That was grown during Oatara if possible, and add compost.

'This is our gift to you! We are grateful for your teaching us the wisdom of silence within and mysteries of how and when to speak and listen."

> Everyone will draw large butterflies to cutout and tie to the trees or ribbons.
> East participant says

'These are our gifts to you! We are honored for you sharing your wisdom Of The subconscious with us and helping us implement these in our lives!

> Sprinkle peat moss in the air for the Earth and add it to the soil in the Earth quarter
> South participant;
> dry flower petals are thrown into the cauldron.

These are our gifts of love to you for sharing and showing us the wisdom to learn when to and not to "pick a fight" and take a stand. For the knowledge you have shared with us, we are appreciative

> West participant
> Water the plant of choice and add fertilizer.

You have shared your wisdom and showed us how to graciously give and receive constructive criticism and alter our faults when faced. For this, we gift continual growth.

Light Spirit flame and say the Great Spirit Words

We invite you, Old Ones of love, light, and darkness, to be with us, and we hope to share in your joy as you in ours.

Let energy flow and sing or chant with dancing around Maypole. The Maypole is within the circle. The pole has a large nail or hooks with a ribbon of festive colors for each participant. The participants are divided in half with ribbons and prepared to dance, skipping around the Maypole to lively music! In one circle, every other participant dances in opposing directions. This wraps the ribbons around the pole during the dance. Many insist on the participants dancing in this method. If you wish to, that's fine. I'll tell you to dance the way you choose. But, using festive music to honor life, I would rather you have fun with life and dance around the pole as you see fit.
Tarot work-play if you choose.
Libations are done in rhyme or sung.
The Sphere must be closed in reverse.

LITHA- SUMMER SOLSTICE

The Summer Solstice is when the sun begins to descend at its peak. When the Oak King of the waxing year, the Sun king relinquishes and is transformed into the Holly King, the God of the waning year.

Some know this as the beginning of the death of Llugh, the Sun king. The Summer Solstice is a time of the Great Fire of this tremendous solar festival. If weather and scheduling permit, it would be appropriate to hold this ritual at high noon. This is an excellent time to bury amulets you have made for beneficial energies and create new ones.

The Cauldron is a crucial tool, symbolizing death and rebirth.

A candle procession with a song is also another solstice activity. This festival has been taken and renamed St. Johns's Day in other traditions. Many people work with corresponding Fey of flora, fauna, and the height of life!!! Reaffirm that water is an essential element! Accompanied by flame., Both for their lifegiving properties. This is a time to gather sacred woods such as Oak, Cedar, and Holly for use in the bonfire or make wands and staffs. Finally, many people revere the Union of the Lady and Lord with celebratory weddings!!

SUMMER SOLSTICE/LITHA RITE

Insert in spell working section of Sphere

Have the altar decorated in gold and brown
Have a red candle on the altar with gold, green, and brown candle
Have a Sun crown on the altar for the Holly King. This is made with brown and gold twigs or flowers interspersed with Holly
Priest/ess lights all candles and says;

The year's wheel turns, bringing us to the height of Summer- Litha! We gather on this Blessed day to celebrate the season of Midsummer. We come to honor the bountiful mother Goddess and benevolent Sun God who rides above us at the peak of his power. We all are part of them, and they are us! We are their children

Priest and priestess don Green Man/Lady cloaks over everything worn. The Priest is wearing a Christmastide cloak underneath his Summer cloak, as in layers Priestess lights gold and red candles, saying:

This is the Summer Solstice, the longest day of the year. Light reigns triumphant yet slowly gives way, changing to dark.

The candles, one by one, are lit. One red, one green, one white, and one yellow.

All repeat

I await the coming of the dawn. As the Sun rises, The Triple Goddess once more gives birth to the Divine Child. In silence and wonder, we stand before the Sacred cauldron of rebirth, knowing we must pass through the cauldron and be reborn.

Pries/tess circles with a white lit candle on the altar

This candle will represent drawing to earth all the balance of the universe.

Priest circles with a lit gold candle on the altar as the priest says

This candle represents all who give us life, balance, and peace. We ask that your hidden wisdom be renewed in us once more!!

All Say

I ask that the eternal power of life accept me. I stand before thee as one whose soul is open. Fill my soul with rebirth that I may see and understand! I ask that a new Spiral be begun.

The Priest Changes the cloak from the Light cloak to the Darker mantle underneath, replacing the Greenman cloak of the lightyear to Christmastide/Dark year's mantle. All discuss the aspects of Litha and what the growing dark and shadow means to them Spiral dancing and continual chanting are good to raise energy and circle Sun wise chanting:

As the new is born, so the old shall die and be reborn!

Sing of choice or story tell
All repeat with the Priest/ess

Great Ones turn the wheel once more

The appointed Goddess steps forward, bathes in the sunlight, and states

The Sun God is transforming into the glorious Dark Lord at this time. Hence we must embrace the darkness in our lives.

The Oak and Holly kings step forward, and the Goddess says:

There can be only one God of the harvest and of the Waning year.

Holly King states:

I am the Holly King, God of the Waning year. Fear not the ravage of summers heat and drought, for I have come to guide you and the Earth to all my blessings.
So I ask you to come into the shadow and embrace the unknown

Priest/ess then says

The Oak King has gone to the under realm. Nevertheless, we shall work together in darkness, for one always requires the opposite in all things.
The Holly King reigns, and our Mother Earth is heavy with the harvest's bounty. This is a reminder that they are with us physically. We are heralding another summer past. The Sun God reaches his zenith and wanes as he transforms into the Dark God.

All:

BLESSED BE
Priestess and Priest return to the altar and face all
As Priestess places the crown on Holly Kings' head, saying

The wheel of the year has turned once again. We are prepared for a new beginning and ending

All repeat with the priestess

We are the children of Deity, one in the spirit of our Goddess and God. So merry meet merry part and meet again.
Blessed be

LUGHNASADH IS-

Lughnasadh is the Festival taking place on the Second of August. It is decidedly Celtic, and Lugh is the god whom this is named for. The energy of Lugh is very passionate and creative, and he is a durable fire deity! Hence, saltpeter and sulfur are used in the fire. Lugh's energy resonates and vibrates on the same frequency as the Seraph Archangel Michael and the Norse Loki fire element. Lughnasadh is the first harvest festival; the primary colors are golds and brown, as the Sun's strength is illustrated. The first crops are used as an adornment on the altar. This festival is done using brown or gold decorations. Bring corn, fruits, vegetables, flowers, sunflowers, Gold and Red Canna Lilies, gold mix marigolds if still in bloom, and any gold or brown life forms to your sacred space. Use your intuition! Gold and yellow candles to represent the Sun are lit; herbs ruled by the Sun are used. A statement of empowerment for all is made. The purpose of the ritual and asking and teaching about LUGH. In your rite's "WORKING" period, insert this if you choose. The Deities worked within this rite have resonance and significance to the working of Lughnasadh. Again, research as you will and trust your intuition.

LUGHNASADH RITE

INSERT IN SPHERE SPELLWORKING

This Festival is done using white or gold adornments. Bring corn, fruits, vegetables, flowers, sunflowers, Gold and Red Canna Lilies, and gold mixed marigolds, if still in bloom, to your sacred space; gold and yellow candles to represent the Sun are lit; herbs ruled by the sun are used. A Statement of empowerment for all is made, and the purpose of the ritual and asking and teaching about Lugh. In your rite's "WORKING" period, insert this Lughnasadh rite if you choose. These words are said firmly with the Sword in hand, raised vertically, aligning with your heart.

Priest-ess says-and all repeat

"I stand in the frontline of battle, king and leader of the land. Long-armed with spear and armor, I stand in the front line of battle.

Pries-ess says

"We gather to celebrate the year's turning and the beginning of the grain harvest. Great Lugh, we honor you."

Light gold and white candles
Elements of the circle are called a bit differently.
QUARTER PEOPLE
East
"I call the Dagda; bring your power and come to this sacred Tara."
East quarter blows smoke, then,
South
"I call Ogma to come in your glory; we welcome you."
South quarter throw saltpeter/sulfur
West
"I call Manannan Mac Lir; bring your power and might
To this, Tara- we welcome you."
West quarter throw water
North
"I call Glorious Lugh to come in your power to this sacred space! We welcome you."
North quarter throw dust
These words are meant to be a reenactment of Lugh's entrance into Tara)
Choose two who will enact the story. One as Lugh, the other as Tara's gatekeeper

"My name is Llugh. I am the son of Cian and the grandson of Balor by Eithne, my mother."
"But what do you do, for no one enters Tara without an art."
"I am a carpenter."
"We don't need a carpenter. We already have one called Luchtaine."
"I am a clever smith."
"We have one of those as well. His name is Goibhniu."
"I am a warrior."
"Ogma is our champion."
"I am a harpist, a poet from the Land of Apples, rich in swans and yew trees."
"We've already an excellent bard."
"I am a sorcerer."
"We've many druids
"I am a healer."
"Our healer is Diancecht."
"I am a cupbearer."
"We've nine of them."

"I am a worker in bronze."
"We've one called Creidni, and he's a very good one too."
"Then go ask Nuada the King if he has a single man who can do all these. If he has, there is no need for me in Tara."

All in the circle pass the sword stating their names and occupations with pride in themselves. Using the blade to empower the food which all intake, All participants circle round the libation foods
Priest/ess-says

"Lugh, great God of the Golden Spear, bringer of the harvest, you are many skilled. So cast your golden light and share it with us."

Priest/ess says

"The magical music of the many spirits has heralded the coming of Lugh. Lugh, strike this blade with your Golden Spear to enter this sovereign place. I draw the golden light of Lugh into this food and drink, which we share with all."

Priestess offers the chalice and food to the God-dess as all charge internally, and libation is given to Deities.

" I call all powers of positive to this Earth. I thank the powers of the Cauldron and the Spear for the bounty we see."

Priest/ess charge herbs, and all repeat

"I speak as Priest/ess to charge these herbs blessed are they, blessed are the grounds from which they grow. we ask that all people of the Earth partake of this bounty".

"Blessed is Lugh, blessed is wise Ogma, blessed is the Dagda."

MEDICRIN

Boy scout troop.com

On my travels, I witnessed these events in the Nordic town of Trinsic.
These people were plagued nightly by a giant beast that would come from hiding in its cave amongst the hills and trees. This beast would take an innocent nightly and devour them. As time went on, the town of Trinsic lost most of its citizens to this beast, and the wise men and women called a council figuring the old Gods had some need, and they knew not how to stop this. All decided that a hero needed to be hired to slay this beast. In the glory of Hercules and Jason, an answer was received.

Erik was the name of the hero who answered their plea to help. Erik was a well-known slayer of horrid beasts in the Northern lands. He, however, was perplexed at hearing of the vile cruelty of this creature, and he replied, "I will seek knowledge to slay this beast for you, fine folk. Erik then went to his training cavern, and as he researched his many books, he found, "This beast is called a Medicrin."

'It loves to feast on human flesh, yet Loons are creatures much to its taste!

Erik searched far and wide through many lands and finally found a Loon. When he brought it to Trinsic, he instructed the townspeople to dig a large pit trapping the Medicrin. Bound in a net, Erik put in the Loon as bait, teaching the few folks left, 'When the Medicrin is in the pit with the Loon, you will trap, bind and slay it. Hence your plague will end, and no more Medicrin.

The Medicrin that eve came down to the town, as it had for many nights before. It smelled the richness of human flesh, yet- it smelled its favorite food to feast on, and heading to the pit of the Loon, the Medicrin also smelled – DANGER, so again he grabbed an innocent of the town and headed back to the black forest whence it came. The townspeople were extremely angered at seeing this," Erik's plan Failed,"

"We demand you to forfeit your life to the Medicrin, or we will," Erik knowing the people would slay him, told him in earnest. "I will find and counsel with my wisest teacher and slay this beast for you all!!!

Erik left in haste, did locate his Master, and sought another weakness for the Medicrin. Erik returned to Trinsic and earnestly told all, "Sugar is critical;" place sugar in the pit! So as he told all in the town what to do, Erik found as much sugar as possible throughout the surrounding villages and made a large sack, placing it in the pit. The Loon was hungry and ate all in the bag at this time. Erik thought- "My life is forfeit. I must steal away now or be hunted. I must save myself." Then Erik did hear a large bustle and growl. The Medicrin returned, and Erik stole away to the tallest tree to see.

The Medicrin smelled the flesh yet again and smelled the Loon, the sack, and its delicious contents. Yes, the smell of danger was about, but the scent of the Loon and sugar was too much, so the beast jumped into the pit, thus devouring the Loon, and was destroyed by the townspeople, who, now rid of the vile beast, were sooo happy!!! When Erik witnessed these events, he climbed down from his tree and let the people of Trinsic know his words of wisdom, telling them, "A LOON FULL OF SUGAR DOTH HELP THE MEDICRIN GO DOWN."

YEARLY PERSONAL RITUALS

As you so choose

RITUAL TIMINGS AND INSERTION

Certain Sabbats and times may have particular guidelines for ease if one wishes to be specific astrology. In addition, some herbs and candles used in certain spells may require waxing or waning moon charges, such as binding and success spell work tools, which get done on the Waxing or Waning moon.

A personal touch is required on many tools, such as Divinatory tools. This requires one to be in constant daily contact with them for some time, such as sleeping with one's tools, the bond between you and the tool gets stronger as you do this more.

In the case of other tools, a person may wish to hold a circle specific to the charging process. In addition to the Lunar charging, you will give to the tool in question.

As Rites/Rituals are primarily Lunar, A reasonable frame of reference/standby rule of thumb is that the differing Moons can be used to time the rituals. One can insert these within the Great Sphere. There are no main rules for the insertion placement, but the spell working time/point of insertion seems best, as this completes Sphere.

MOON MAGICK

There are many forms of moon magick. A person has only to use intuition, for that is what the moon may be telling you.

NEW OR WAXING MOON,

In simplest terms, the New Moon is a time for growth or gain. Many tool consecrations may be completed within this period. This is an excellent time for ritual-charging herbs. Much Earth Magick is done as this is the time of the Maiden Goddess to invoke prosperity and abundance. There are many ways to do this. Creating a handcrafted work of what you wish, anything with a personal touch will bring the most power. Keep a Book of Shadows, if you choose, for you will want to record how everything magically worked for you.

THE FULL MOON

The most potent moon that we see. A Blue Moon is even more magical. It is the second Full moon in a month, which accounts for 13 full moons in 365 days. You may want to charge or bless what you will. This is the prime time to do it. Use a creative visualization with your tools and draw the Moon's energy into you. This is the peak of the Mother Goddesses so invoke them. Any work you begin at the New moon should come to pass during a Full moon, but always be realistic and give things some time. A Lunar Sabbat such as Samhain and Beltane are more than mere nights. They are periods when one can feel the veils between the world's opening.

DARK – WANING MOON PERIOD

This is a time from the last day of the Full Moon t the night before the New. This is a period of the Crone and Dark Mother. All bindings, banishings, and magick are done in this period to eliminate something. The Waning Moon is when most dark works can be done, yet beware of Karma's threefold law. In the dark half of the year, this is very potent and a prime time for Shadow work, Getting rid of the old and starting new with the New moon. Many traditions cast a Dark moon circle for added protection at this time. The Lunar year has many names for its periods of the full moons

JANUARY -WOLF MOON
FEBRUARY-CHASTE MOON
MARCH-SEED MOON

APRIL-HARE MOON
MAY-FAERY MOON
JUNE-HOLLY MOON
JULY-MEAD MOON
AUGUST- BARLEY MOON
SEPTEMBER- WINE MOON
OCTOBER- BLOOD MOON
NOVEMBER-BIRCH MOON
DECEMBER-OAK MOON

INCENSES AND THEIR MANY USES

There are many types of Incense to use for many purposes. A very popular is smudging- It is a practice that clears negative energy by utilizing many herbs. Cedar, and Sage, are the most prominent for smudging. Smudging, if it is needed, is very simple. Take the herb, and burn it to release the smoke. Snudging, in some form, SHOULD help the energy leave or dissipate. An oil diffuser is just as effective with particular oils. Additionally, plant incenses/ energies are beneficial for Earthly powers as they are Earthly.

There are many reasons a thing is as it is. Many teachers understand and work magic and may have specific results (this helps you know you are on the right track). However, these effects/results remain the same. Throughout history, Mages have utilized the same techniques with cultural differences. I only reiterate what I can!

One should always understand the intended goal and use smudges accordingly to reach that goal. Use your intuition and speak with the energies of the incense in question. They will speak in kind to you!

Sage is a great "right now" Smudge, as is Cedar. However, as with many Earthly- plants, their clearing powers may only work on worldly matters, and much energy is universal. Smudging is effective in clearing a space of unwanted energy. They are of Earthly power! For example, a beginner or one who does not know may be affected by smudging. If they have extraordinary abilities, their energy may be denser; it is sometimes helpful to use a plant-metal-resin mixture to attain denser working.

Sage is excellent as a very light clearing during the Waxing moon. It may not be 100% and last for only a bit, yet the problem will continue to affect the things in question. Cedar is denser energy and can help against chaotic Earthly beings, most effectively used during a waning moon.

Any Plant may be used for smudge, lily, pine, marigold/calendula, etc. These listed are very common. It is of great benefit to use these in combination with others.

Resin scents cross energetic boundaries as they are both earthly and other/aiding in clearing universal energies. I have listed some of the most common.

FRANKINCENSE

extremely dense yet Light-Divine energy. This will bring in Divine powers to overcome the negative and clear. Frankincense is very solar energy. This is good to use in combination with almost any other incense.

MYRRH

This is a Dense yet, dark- or lunar energy. This also brings in many divine powers of differing sorts, dense and dark. These sacred energies will also help clear the space of negativity.

COPAL

It is its neutral energy as well. This is not only of Divine power but of Fey as well. This has no polarity- solar or lunar as it is neutral.

DRAGONS BLOOD

A dense resin, but it affects earthly and universal totems/energies. Dragon's Blood is mainly used in addition to other incense as it has great strength to add a power boost to what incense you are working with as it is multi-dimensional. It has a tremendous effect during the Waning moon/New moon period.

PINE

This resin does have many dense Earthly ties as it helps against or brings about totemic energies of this realm and others, depending on the mix and goal.

CINNAMON

This is a very positive, divine, healing solar scent. It attracts very comforting and wholesome energies. It has been used for that reason and is associated with the Samhain/Yule periods of the year.

CLOVE

A very positive yet dark lunar scent. This energy demands stillness and contemplation. The action only comes when things, peace, and reflection are attained. It is very effective against chaotic, confusing energies.

Multidimensional effects on all planes are created with the vibrational effects of metal!

I understand this is unusual, but through much theoretical physics study, I have learned this to be an easily accessible way to create lasting change. On a grand scale, I ask that one speak or commune with each metal, as each energy's details will be communicated.

IRON

The primarily used element does not harm anyone or faeries, as most people mistakenly believe. Iron is of the Earth so ask yourself why it would hurt anything but lousy energy. It is very grounding. By this, I mean it mainly is felt to resonate with the material realm and create the effect in Iron's unique way. Iron has been added to Incense to generate a charge of intended energy throughout realms, affecting them. So this is a _very_ extreme working/ incense. Well, it is no longer incense per se. It is now a functional spiritual element with material effects. Iron may be acquired in Iron ore, shavings/ Lodestone, Pyrite, Hematite and Magnets, and Boji Stones for their electrical impact on the material.

COPPER

Copper is easy to acquire. It is airy and spiritual in nature. Copper does have a higher vibration than Iron. It is recommended to work with Iron before copper, As iron absorbs all negative energy. Perhaps finish with copper, as it is an excellent conductor of all positive energy. One of the metals will create a spiritual/light/Divine vibration, primarily if used together once negativity is cleared.

LEAD

Please use caution when working with this!
Lead's charge is so unique that it holds or traps any current or previous livelihood energy. Therefore, lead may be used in any banishings or bindings one wishes to make permanent. Consider this wisely, for it will be endless! Lead can be found in fishing weights.

GOLD

A very conductive and resistant metal to solar/aggressive/protective charge-vibration. This is used for adding charge/ vibration to a person or space. People enjoy wearing this for this purpose. Gold is found in either rose, white or yellow.

SILVER

Silver is the best conductor of electrically charged energy. Silver also reflects or sends back power to its immediate origin, cyclical. This metal people will adorn themselves with for these reasons.

Other ritual additions

GYPSUM/SULFUR

Throw in flames for the electric blue effect! It also is a form of acquiring magical attention from Deities! Just be careful! Understand it stinks- It is a form of brimstone!

HIGH PROOF SPIRITS

Bacardi 151, or Ever clear, is a liquid used to create the Spirit Flame! One can, in a pinch, use Isopropyl alcohol!

An essential Draconic incense for use during basic circles or cleansing I will leave recipes for these different incenses in the recipe section of this book, and one should understand their basics.

MIRROR MAGICK

Mirrors are doorways to other realms and dimensions. Mirrors can be dangerous if misused. However, mirrors can be charged for specific reasons and can help us in many ways, Such as sending energy back to whence it came or radiating what power was sent.

Mirrors have been used for divination for many thousands of years. They take many forms, such as water, metal, or stone. A natural mirror will have much easier access to the Faery realm than a store-bought mirror. A mirror made by one's hand from natural items is the most potent above all.

A dark or black mirror is primarily used for Dark Crone or Dark Lord magick A mirror is always handmade. On the other hand, a light mirror will attract many spirits, and both types will attract many estranged entities. So I highly recommend one know their action before working this form of magick. Hence one may not wish to place a mirror in one's entryway. It is highly recommended to charge specific mirrors according to their use.

HUMAN MAGNETISM

Charisma, love& confidence are magnetic. Therefore, people flock to the person of Honor who wishes to attract these "young-minded" persons and give them a knowledgeable view of things they can use to enhance their lives!

People with a moral attitude and outlook on the proper "future" need to radiate this, for it may be confused as arrogance or wrongful pride. So please take a second look; these people are helping others and have magnetic personalities. However, a truly magnetic personality is not always just easily given. Sometimes we have to work for it.

To lead many in an honorable fashion, we must be like the "Pied Piper" and make others genuinely want to be around us. Leading by example, many people will come if we radiate love and caring with our charisma. If people fear approaching us, our love and caring help break the barrier!

APPOINTMENT IN SAMARRA

CELEBRATE THE DARKNESS

Why do a dark ritual? All the universe's energies should be worked with as best as possible! These rituals enhance one with the dark powers, enfolding all life. A dark ritual can be started as early as the day after the full moon and as late as the night before the new moon. V/C moons are highly beneficial at this time as well!

DARK RITE

One astral candle is needed per participant consecrated with one drop of blood. An astral candle represents the practitioner and is a smaller candle used for this ritual only. It can be of any color the practitioner identifies with. Let the blood dry, and let the candles mold together. Next, a syringe /needle is used to get blood mixed with consecration oil for the circle. Call quarters to protect. If you like, insert this rite into your complete ritual. Or you can use SPHERE as a whole ritual!

East-
Powers of the east, please grant us your knowledge and protection.

South-
Powers of the south, please grant us your guidance.

West-
Powers of the west, give us your great wisdom.

North-
Please grant us your power –

We are here to reconnect with the universal energies and the dark arts to learn from all dark arts teachers.

Great rite

Place a bit of each other's blood and rub
it around each other's breast.
Together we come to reconnect with the dark arts; please show us the correct ways to gain knowledge, understanding, and power of the arts so we may become better adept at using them for the good of most. We ask to be one and understand the dark dragons and the laws of the universe.

North
Depart in peace o powers of the North

West
Depart in peace o powers of the West

South
Depart in peace o powers of the South

East
Depart in peace o powers of the East

BLOOD OATH RITE

This rite is done when a person wishes to state their strength and intent of following the exemplified path to the universe and Universal spirits. You are telling the universe that you will uphold these ways of life and defend them to your fullest ability. A Blood Oath Rite is best done with a witness to your action. Blood will be used as a blood sister/brother. The easiest way to get your blood is with a diabetic needle or a sewing needle inserted in an eraser and let it bounce till acquired.

SELF-DEDICATION/BLOOD OATH RITE

Cast- If one wishes, this rite can be inserted in the spell-working portion of sphere.

Center light and Greet saying:

May all within this sacred sphere gain the wisdom and understanding of spirit.
 O fair and magical Freja Loki and Lilith, we light these flames in thy honor. Dearest wise ones, Draconics of old, Help us know the importance of balancing our lives with seriousness, play, order, and chaos. We do ask of thee this day! Loki, Lilith, share your eternal wisdom and knowledge of the universal laws of chaos and balance with us. Show us how to bring these into our lives so we can use them wisely!

CODE of HONOR WORDS
DRAGONHEART Universal pictures/1998

(name) KNOWS ONLY AND IS SWORN TO VALOR
MY HEART KNOWS ONLY VIRTUE
MY BLADE DEFENDS THE HELPLESS
MY MIGHT UPHOLDS THE WEAK
MY WORD SPEAKS ONLY TRUTH
MY WRATH UNDOES THE WICKED

This I swear to live by
With my sister Lilith mistress and teacher of magicks
To my brother Loki master and teacher
of sacred Draconic Wyrd
To all universal Draconii in our midst and beyond, I swear
any bloodlust and tyranny left within me die now
I promise to help with mercy
I will come with you, my dear brother, lovely sister, and
learn the once ways with you together as one we shall
be as these secrets learned I might pass on wisely
This, I do swear!
I ask your strength to purify my weaknesses. As
I swear these oaths, this shall be done now!
Call when you need me, ask what you will of
me, my sword, my service is yours!

Drink charged water and wine.

O great ones of beauty and sensuality, we work this rite in thy honor with warm blessings. Grant us that which we desire

When all is done, say

We thank you, Ancient ones, for your aid and
wisdom. We invite you to join our celebration!

Priest/ess circle around to all

May you never hunger
May you never thirst

Three times round toast with all is made. Thanks to the elements is done in reverse. Dark ice cream, chocolates, and ale for libations

Depart in peace o powers of
South fire, east air, north earth, west water
To all visible and invisible beings, we thank you for your aid in this rite! Merry meet merry part, and merry meet again.

Uncast

ATHENA DISCUSSION

Why do anything for Athena? Many people have many reasons. The most basic is that one resonates with Greek deities to the few who understand Athena's mysteries. Athena/Minerva is an aspect of an ancient triad of sisters. Many know these sisters as the Norns, good fairies, three witches, Wyrd sisters, weaves, and very well.

Her main totem, besides the owl, shares its wisdom in helping Athena gain insight. And the spider, for as the spider, she accesses the many deep realms of the universe and its many secrets. Athena also uses many unusual tactics to teach others. Like the Norns, she is critical of those who work with the Wyrd and their traditions. Athena is the light, simple-to-understand version of the complex Lilith. Again this ritual is meant to be inserted in the spell-working section of Sphere.

Athena Rite

Prepare the altar with rose, blue royal, yellow-orange, and white minis. Any decoration you may find appropriate will be appropriate. Use a Queen of Heaven-type incense. Using the rite, have a snake or spider in some life form. Even skin or web is possible. Athena likes them.

This ritual is inserted in the Sphere. This is at the start of the Sphere.

Statement of Athenas invoking and each person share what they know about her.

INVOCATION TO ATHENA

The winds are rising, and with them, I ask for the presence of Goddess Athena!

Hail Athena, Goddess of air, wisdom, and battle! Lady of the freshening wind and the illuminating dawn. Thou who art the cutting edge of thought. Grant me this As we may make our way through this world. Please show us the path of pride in my work and success in my craft. Give to me with your shining blade of grace and will. Grant me the awareness, ability, and enthusiasm I need so that my efforts will always serve as a testament to your patronage as you judge me with wisdom.

Blessed be Athena.

SPIDER RITE

Creative Weaver of Fate

Spider totems teach balance --
between past and future, physical and spirit,
Male and female.
She is strong and gentle combined.
She awakens creative sensibilities
and reminds you that the past is always interwoven
with the future.

Godmother with tea serves each person.
Godmother serves apple chips and cotton candy s well.
Cotton candy symbolizes the web of Spider.

May you never hunger – May you never thirst

All share stories, such as Frau Holle and Anansi. All share sharing an understanding of magic.
Three times round toast with all is made. Thanks to the elements is done in reverse.

Depart in peace o powers of West and water. We give thanks to you for your aid in this Rite!

In turn also, South, Fire- East, Air- North, Earth- West, Water
Return to altar.

To all beings of the Visible and Invisible, we thank you for your aid in this rite! Merry Meet, Merry Part, and Merry Meet again!

Uncast

The Sphere is open, yet not broken! Forever it remains a Sphere. Around and through us flows its Magic always!

LILITH

Many people have preconceived ideas about who they know as Lilith. Hence, she does exist in mythology and biblically; however, I will not delve into theology. That would make this short description an entire book. Instead, I want to share what she shared with me and shed some light on her mythology and the actions she has been accused of. Lilith is one of the oldest deities in creation. She is not just a Deity but Dragoness, Noble Faery, Vampyre, and Death walker. She is the guardian of what many call female rights and concerns, Divine sex, Orgasm Magic, and Ritual sex. She is the Original feminist, for she would not submit to Adam as he wanted in the Book of Genesis.

However, many do not realize that Lilith wants one to embrace their full power and understand they do not need the help of another to attain their full strength. Lilith works very well with Loki, who is also not what many assume him to be. He is a Trickster but not a fool or one who plays practical jokes. A Trickster will only foul up one's life to show those working with them that they can overcome their problems independently and find their strength. A Trickster will know this is a challenge the person in question can overcome- it is just something done to prove to a person they are capable of more than they know.

It is as if they are saying, "See, I will prove to you. You CAN do this on your own" these Deities are concerned with aiding people to find their self-strength and not relying on others to do for them what they can do themselves. Lilith will only come to one who is ready, for she is very dense, and many find her unappealing. Her light form is what many know as Blodeuwedd or Athena.

Lilith is a very dense Faery Queen, yet she is not easy for many to work with. Lilith is "Very Nasty," showing how self-orgasm and masturbation lead to personal power and growing strength. In doing so, embracing and remaining mindful of the Divine Spiritual realm and self-growth within it is of utmost importance. This is solemn work, and one's mind must be focused and unwavering on this for growth and wisdom to come. Lilith is a Sumerian/Babylonian

Deity. And as the Jewish fathers detested any woman with power or strength, this wasn't very good. Hence the prejudiced mindset of the current age.

One may use these sacred words in addition to the Spellworking addition to Sphere.

Dearest Lilith, we ask you to partake in our lives! You, the one that bears wisdom of all physical and emotional love and lust.

Fill our souls with knowledge and understanding. Help us know the importance of balancing our lives with reverent bliss!

CLEANSING RITE

This ritual cleans any negative entities in space and living areas. Smudging rarely helps rid strong energy. The iron stakes attract all negative energy and trap it. When this is done, these MUST be buried in an unused area of the North. So they do not find a way to wreak havoc. One wants a permanent death and further imprisonment of these energies. Trust me; they will try!! Use lead, but please do not touch it! It will trap and render ALL energy void, and Returning to normal after this will be extremely hard.

Follow this burial with the magnetism of attracting good energies to your area by inserting copper stakes in the ground in each of the four directions in a deosil /sunwise manner. Insert this into Draconis sphere, or it can be done alone.

O mighty Dragons of old
Dear Lady and Lord, we are joined with trusted friends to banish the discouraging, confusing energy of old; we___ understand and know that your way is that of love, trust, and respect. We___ are tired and wish to banish from our presence those whose energies we find of unlove falsehood and disrespect of your path in their lives. We --- no longer wish this.

-All throw light-throwing motion with intent
"With this light, be gone."

We __ ask old ones who give the breath of life, creativity, knowledge, and wisdom and grant these gifts to be bestowed upon this sacred space in our home.

(With these actions, meditate and focus thoughts on what you wish to be done)
All throw white Air

We ask dear wise ones who warm and comfort all creation with balanced action, grant that these gifts be bestowed on this sacred space of our __ home

All throw orange Fire

We ask dearly loved, mighty ancient ones who gently cleanse our hearts, minds, and souls. Through all creation, we ask that you aid in cleansing this sacred space of our __ home

All throw blue Water energy

We ask o, great powerful ones of solidity who ground and protect all, to grant your blessings of stability to ground our sacred space, our --- home!

All throw green Earth energy

We ask o righteous Dragons, dear Lady and Lord, positive spirits of this sacred space, our__ home, which aids us in cleansing this night.

All come into the house working clockwise circularly yet not crossing the triangle, then moving to the other side around, saying as each room is smudged, chimed flamed, spritzed,

"I Cleanse this Space with my might!"

After each room is left, finish with,

> "So mote it be."

When done inside, bring out the salt triangle and
burn the entire thing with all old negativity
Prepared iron stakes are then cooled, set in water,
and passed through incense with words to strengthen
the barrier as they are hammered in place.

Build and strengthen this barrier for peace of mind, body, and soul! Keep at bay all hostile unloving forces that wish to do Harm!

Once all stakes are in place, say any peace words of choice
Then open the circle

WHAT IS CROSSING??

Some people or spirits have chosen not to embrace the plane that awaits them. The living in grieving may be holding on to the memory of their loved one and not letting them go, and this is where Copal and Myrrh may help. Some spirits, when passed on, still choose to remain here and not move onto the next plane tormenting many innocents. They need help, hence Crossing aiding Rite. The Rite could be coupled with the Samhain Rite in the Yearly Sabbat section.

CROSSING INSTRUCTIONS

The altar is set with mirrors, and crossroads are excellent for this as Hecate loves them. Natural soil is best. Otherwise, use mirrors.
    Copal, Myrrh, Dragons Blood, and Cinnamon are suitable incense. Have a cauldron with fluid circled with candles for the deceased. The liquid should be ocean water only as it is between realms. Blood? Only if you feel it is necessary. It is good to utilize, but there are many other ways to do this.
    When invoked, use candles to represent Hecate, Lilith, Cernunnos, and Scairon (SHARON). Crow or Raven feathers also aid in lifting the veil and passing thru.

This is mostly energy working. The person involved needs to understand the needs of the spirit they need to help cross so that communication may be more manageable. Here are suggestions of words that have been used in the verbal aspect of the rite. I'll take it from the center so one may understand how I have worked it.

I recommend doing this inside a more significant rite, not isolating itself!

CROSSING AID RITE

It can be done solely or inserted into "Sphere."

May all within this Sacred Sphere gain the wisdom and understanding of spirit. Within and encompassing our universes known and unknown, guard this Sphere and be with all, bringing forth knowledge, pearls of wisdom, and understandings of order and chaos to be felt and known. Give your aid to this rite!

Let energy flow and sing or chant priest/ess, then states.

We consecrate this place of rite with salt, water, smoke, and firelight, This sphere is bound with power all around between the worlds we stand with protection at hand.

-Invoking of HECATE AND OTHER DARK DEITIES est.'s done priest/ess complete with an invoking pentagram, then say the PASSING WORDS
Hand washing and Sprinkling

I am washing the grief and unhappiness away from your spirit. As the water cleanses your hands and you are sprinkled, it may cleanse your whole being
A statement of intent is made depending on the situation, and the working is done. The message can be a time of teaching for all members as well
When all is done, say

Loki, Lilith, Hecate, Sscairon, and Cernunnos, guardians of the Gates of Death, we_ request that you open the gates that _may pass for a final communion. Great guardians -is ready to join you now and depart our world.

Quiet listening with the deceased is done before they cross over Motion to open the veil, circle widdershins. With Copal and Myrrh. Extinguish altar cauldron candles widdershins. As well All touch the ground and connect to the Earth before releasing circle
Depart in peace o powers of the West and water, and we thank you for your aid in this rite! Water West/ south Fire/East air/north Earth
Return to altar
To all visible and invisible beings, we thank you for your aid in this rite! Merry meet merry part, and merry meet again.
Uncast
The Sphere is open yet not broken. It continually remains a Sphere, and through us flows its magic always!

LOVE AND HAPPINESS

Many people wonder "Why a "Valentine's ritual" Saint Valentine has many violent implications. One can dwell on the negative or celebrate what St. Valentine lived for. Lupercalia may have origins on this date, but it is very unrelated. My argument is that the world calendar has changed so much that minor rites like this one have no constraint, and a person may choose to celebrate this small ritual of love!

A person's likes and dislikes must be taken to be critical here because if something is a chore, the energy is polluted!

This rite can be inserted in your main ritual and the spell working insertion.

An annual Valentine's rite.

VALENTINES

Prepare the altar with rose petals sprinkled on and around. Dove feathers, pastel love candles of yellow, pink, bright red, lavender, and such; use Jasmine flowers or incense if possible.

All say;

Ancient queens of old! Branwen, Aine, Aphrodite, Venus, Inanna, you who keep love sacred and well for all life!
We have come before you to partake in Love! May we honor you all in this paradoxical emotion essential to all life! We—(insert name) wish to share with you the mysteries and festivities that we may partake in the growth of love in our lives!
My soul is longing; lead me to spiritual harmony.
My mind lies dormant; fill it with fertility.

Write your spell on paper cutout in the shape of hearts, and when done, hold them aloft once oiled and/or censed, say:

Let a bond of love hold us fast through time and space— drawing us forward until we stand face to face—within this sacred space, hidden from the world outside of time and free of control by man. So may we worship in this Sacred center and work with the Old ones again! Love in all its many forms, sweetness, joy, and delight, Bless us, sweet ladies, and brighten each new night!

INVOKING RITE

This very small rite cleans the area of any harmful vibrations. It uses copper to attract beneficial energies. Burn Invoking incense and uses black and white candles. Saying The PRAYER AND PLAY WORDS in the Sacred words section.

I am calling to the spirits
I call to the spirit of laughing water,
I call to the spirit of the singing wind,

I call to the spirit of dancing fire and the spirit of the drumming Earth.

Sing of the mountain prince for a day. I call all beneficial deities with positive universal energies to aid me in attracting strength and love.

Peace, wisdom, and universal magic within this space of ever-growing.

Come wild, Rogue, frolicsome Maid.

Merry with magic, remind us how to be children when play was our worship, and pleasure our prayer. Let us laugh ourselves silly and throw our cares to the wind.

Let mirth be our magic and humor our hymn. I ask for new beginnings, ideas, wisdom, and guidance to act upon all found within this sacred space.

Let beauty, joy, relaxation, and love radiate and attract as a magnet; all that it does as a mirror reflects for all who enter this Sacred space—taking love, strength, and peace within themselves.

O great guardians, Deities of the ever-spiraling womb of all universal life, I create this Sacred Sphere in your honor!

We always ask that you share the wisdom of all balance, respecting, and blissfulness. Ever strong yet patient.

Into this space now and ever-growing in strength, it does

Now you are ready to work or complete your invoking as you need.

LOKI

Also, for insertion in the spell-working portion of Sphere.

Why do a ritual involving Loki? He is an ancient universal Deity and a Trickster like the Norns, Spider, and Lilith. A Trickster teaches lessons in a very unusual, roundabout way that hurts. A Trickster teaches that it is necessary to follow or not follow specific rules and directions- understanding what is needed. Many beings we may think of as evil or harmful are sometimes Tricksters, so step aside, and look/think. Their main message is "nothing is as it seems." They break unnecessary rules, and many think they are unruly. These beings, however, are extraordinarily honorable and very trustworthy. This is one of the many things that define a Trickster over an evil spirit. I choose to work with Loki as a primary deity, for he works well with me.

Loki incense is made with mandrake Patchouli, Clove, Cinnamon, Pine, Dragons Blood, and coyote or fox hair.

This is much like Lilith spell used earlier in this chapter.

Dear friend Loki, we ask you to come into our lives! You, the one that bears wisdom of all that flows eternally, fill our souls with knowledge and understanding! Help us know the importance of balancing our lives with reverent bliss, seriousness and play, order, and chaos. So we do ask of thee this day!

FAERY RITE

This is a ritual that can be done by itself and used in place of Sphere

Ritual will be done with a bird out in the circle area, a spider as well, any Fey creature, a circle with votives, and in between will be small glasses with whiskey or scotch.

Libations will be sung or stated in rhyme, and green apples and iced tea; for all the wicked stepmothers and good fairies. This Rite can be done at any phase of the moon and most deities. This Rite can be done in unison or by combining the Beltane, or Spider/Norn Rite, as there are very few differences. The Norns are the eldest Faeries. Plants and animals are the symbols here.

Cast-
The circle is cast with each person carrying each
treasure, spear, sword, stone, cauldron
All enter and make a palm circle
Maiden helps all start song of choice
North
Planting of Honeysuckle

'This is our gift to you! We are grateful for your teaching us the wisdom of silence within and mysteries of how and when to speak and listen."

East
Everyone will draw large butterflies to cutout
and tie to the trees or ribbons

"These are our gifts to you! We are honored for you sharing your wisdom of the subconscious with us and helping us to implement these in our lives!"

Sprinkle peat moss in the air for the earth
South
Build a small fire, and dry flower petals
were thrown into the cauldron

"These are our gifts of love to you for your sharing showing us the wisdom to learn when to and not to "pick a fight" and take a stand. For the wisdom you have shared with us, we are appreciative."

West
Water the Honeysuckle

**You have shared your wisdom and showed us how to graciously give and receive constructive criticism and alter our faults when faced. For this, we gift continual growth
Spirit flame lit.
We invite you old ones of love, light, and darkness to be with us, and we hope to share in your joy as you in ours**

-Charge lit charcoal and incense-use any leaves-mint or Patchouli circle With incense, and surround the area. Let energy flow and sing or chant with dancing, Do Tarot work-play. Libations are done in rhyme or sung. Space must be closed in reverse.

Depart in peace o powers of West and water. We give thanks to you for your aid in this Rite!

Close in order, South fire, East air, North earth

Meet merry part, and bright meet again.

Uncast

The Sphere is open yet not broken forever it remains a sphere; through us flows its magic always!

PETS

Many people wonder why they or others like to have pets. Some people need assistance in daily chores, emotional support, or to feel animals' energy. Some people have pets symbolic of personal totems, as in Druidic, Native American, or astrological/Spiritual. These paths and animal energy help communicate with other worlds/ dimensions. Stillness and listening are essential to be done. A pet/ animal may perform unique behaviors that serve as messages. Again silence and listening are a must. A pet/ animal may bond with you instantly as if to say, "I like you" Totems will always do the same. Is your pet a totem?

Many animals in the wild will come into your personal living space as a message to you. Not everyone ascribes to this practice, but it is no less valid. Obsessing over an animal is just as ridiculous! Some unique behavior may happen to you as a message from the animal world telling you they feel safe. A bee swarm is peaceably inhabiting your space, a bat flying into your house, anything unique. One does not need to be an "animal person" to attract and enjoy animal energy. These people should not be judged, as well. This is one aspect of the power of life that many respond to. Another popular factor is that of plants. They both are excellent communicators of energy. They will send messages to us through their living patterns. Communicating the needs, one must attend to

TOTEMS OF ANIMAL, PLANT, AND SPIRITUAL

I can not go into all totems, but remember that any animal or plant may be totemic.

These are some springtime examples. These totems are sacred and used by many different Deities. Listen to the spirits, for they present messages. Usually appearing in strange unusual places and ushering messages, these are temporary totems. Listen to the earth's energies, for they also conduct messages.

SPRINGTIME ANIMAL EXAMPLES

Swan - This is sacred to the moon and all muses.
Rabbit or Hare - is sacred to Ostara, symbolizing the rebirth of the earth and a moon symbol.
Goose - Laid the golden egg symbolizing the Goddess who gave birth to the sun.
Owl - Sacred to Blodeuwedd- the Goddess of flowers and change. The owl is also a sacred symbol of wisdom, as it is holy to Athena and shares its wisdom with her.
Serpent, snake. Symbolizes the Universal Spiralling energy, A constant reminder of death and rebirth, of life. The snake represents the first level of wisdom on the universal level.
Dove – is sacred to the Great Goddess/Lilith and is also a symbol of feminine sexuality and freedom.
Raven - sacred to the crone Goddesses, and it is a symbol of darkness
Stag - a symbol of the masculine Life, The Green Man. It is also a symbol of male freedom of life and new growth.
Wolf - symbolizes physical strength and wisdom.
Coyote - symbolizes creative strength and wisdom, a trickster.
Peacock - symbolic of seeing or awareness. This is sacred to Juno.
Dog, or lupine species - is a symbol of loyalty and is sacred to Deities of Healing,
Cat, feline species - symbolizes cleverness by stealth. It represents the powers of prophecy and aligns with the moon.
Butterfly - is a symbol of happiness, joy, and laughter during work. Enjoy life! These are sacred to Blodeuwedd.
Horse - is sacred to Epona, and the horse is among the noblest creatures on Earth.
Birds - are givers of enlightenment and bringers of omens.

PLANT TOTEM EXAMPLES

Lavender -Brings calmness, renewal, and love!
Mint - Brings abundant energy and calming, effective grounding herb.
Basil - A protective exorcism plant.
Rosemary - Brings mental clarity and is sacred to all Fey.
Rose - A flower of Great Goddesses.

Lily - Sacred to spring Goddesses and Lilith. This flower has powerful sexual symbolism.
Lilly of the Valley - Said to be faerie bells and carries messages.

There are many sacred trees to the Celts. They are used in Ogham. Birch, Rowan, Alder, Willow, Ash, Hawthorn, Oak, and Holly are sacred trees. Hazel Apple Vine, Ivy, Reed, Blackthorn, Elder, Silver Fir, Furze. Also, Mistletoe, White Poplar/Aspen, Yew, Grove, Spindle, and Beech.

There are other sacred flowers used in the creation of Blodeuwedd. Primrose for protection, Broom for wind spells, Meadowsweet for love, and Cockle. Also, Nettle for exorcism and protection, Thorn, and Chestnut.

SPIRITUAL TOTEMS

Basilisk-
The Basilisk is associated with menstrual blood and is said to grow from the buried hair of a menstruating woman.
Centaur-
They are warriors and very lusty creatures as well.
Kachina/Faery-
Nature spirits govern a specific aspect of the natural world.
Unicorn-
Represents innocence and purity.
Pegasus-
Represents nobility and strength.
Phoenix-
Represents the resurrection and Solar energy.
Dragon-
The first primary being of Universal Energy.

Remember, a totem-spirit guide chooses you. Never you it!

WESTERN NATIVE AMERICAN BIRTH TOTEMS/ZODIAC

Native American culture has always been heavily influenced by nature. Most tribes hold nature as a sacred part of life. People familiar with the western zodiac often want to know if Native Americans have a similar concept. The short answer is yes. Although the animals and meanings are vastly different from the zodiac most people are familiar with, the Native American zodiac describes the nature of a person's personality based on the hemisphere and date they were born.

The core philosophy of Native American birth totems is connectivity. People are connected to the universe, the stars, and nature. What Native American astrology seeks to illustrate is this connection, which can be hard to see as we go about our daily lives in the modern era.

One key difference between the western zodiac and native astrology is its multifaceted nature. The Native American zodiac takes into account numerous pieces of astronomical data to provide people with a deeper understanding of the animal that represents who they are.

The Goose
Dec 22 - Jan 19
Birthstone: Quartz
People that have the Goose as their birth totem seek spiritual enlightenment and tend to have a stoic nature. The Goose is a persevering spirit that's ambitious and driven.

The Otter
Jan 20 - Feb 18
Birthstone: Turquoise
These people are creative and unconventional. The Otter animal totem is set apart by its unique problem-solving method. People born during this time of the year are seen as independent. They try to better the world around them through their methods.

Wolf
Feb 19 - Mar 20
Birthstone: Jade
People with the Wolf birth totem are passionate and deeply emotional. The Wolf is unique because it seeks compassion and understanding but prefers independence.

The Falcon
Mar 21 - Apr 19
Birthstone: Opal
The Falcon is a symbol of wisdom and inspiration. People that have the Falcon as their totem share this passion for truth and knowledge. People born during this time are natural-born leaders who should be sought after for their judgment and wisdom.

The Beaver
Apr 20 - May 20
Birthstone: Jasper
A master strategist and a force to be reckoned with for completing any goal, people with the Beaver birth totem take charge and can quickly adapt to new environments. In addition, people associated with the Beaver are known to have razor-sharp wit.

The Deer/Stag
May 21 - June 20
Birthstone: Agate
Gentle-natured peacemakers, the Deer birth totem, signifies passionate and empathetic people. People born in this timeframe find it easy to connect with new people and are usually the life of the party.

The Woodpecker
June 21 - July 21
Birthstone: Rose Quartz
Known for their sense of community and nurturing instinct, people with the Woodpecker birth totem are empathetic and good at listening to others.

The Salmon
July 22 - Aug 21
Birthstone: Carnelian
Some of the most creative and focused people have the Salmon as their birth totem. This <u>sign</u> embodies generosity, brilliance, and gifted intuition.

The Bear
Aug 22 - Sept 21
Birthstone: Amethyst
The Bear birth totem is often associated with level-headed thinking and a capacity to see the bigger picture. People with this sign are generous and have big hearts.

The Raven
Sept 22 - Oct 22
Birthstone: Azurite
Gifted with deep <u>clairvoyance</u> and foresight, the Raven symbolizes intelligence and charm. People that were born in the time of the Raven share similar attributes.

The Snake
Oct 23 - Nov 22
Birthstone: Copper
The Snake is more deeply connected to the spiritual world than any other animal totem. As a result, people born in this timeframe possess great supernatural power and are often associated with enhanced healing and leadership skills.

The Owl
Nov 23 - Dec 21
Birthstone: Obsidian
A messenger to the Great Spirit and a seeker of truth and wisdom, the Owl is an adventurous spirit with a light-hearted nature. People born in the time of the Owl are often artistic, reckless, and versatilely gifted.

KACHINA FIRE RITUAL

I had the fortunate experience of learning Native American Shaman teachings. As a result, I interpret Native American Kachinas as the many faeries we know.

We gather here this night in union with our relations, the elements, and spirits. We join in honor and celebration with

our sister Kachina Fire Dancer! May your ancient wisdom aid us through our great journey!

Song and dance of choice is led the candle in the east is lit and offering made.

O great ones of the East! I welcome you and ask for your aid in our planting, and the ever-growing wisdom sister Kachina fire dancer has to share with us! With this, we give thanks!

Throw offering, tobacco, or plant ruled by the element of fire
Light the candle of the south, and an offering made

O great ones of the South! I welcome you and ask for your aid in our planting, and the ever-growing wisdom sister Kachina fire dancer has to share with us! With this, we give thanks!

Throw offering of cornmeal.
Light the candle of the West.
Make Offering.

O Great Ones of the West! I welcome you and ask for your aid in our planting, and the ever-growing wisdom sister Kachina fire dancer has to share with us! With this, we give thanks!

Light the candle of North and state

O, Great Ones of the North! I welcome you and ask for your aid in our planting and the ever-growing wisdom sister Kachina Fire Dancer has to share with us! With this, we give thanks!

Throw sage.
Hold the Fire Dancer doll aloft.

O, Great sister! We come together in honor of your sacred wisdom and partake in what you have to share. Let us listen as you do so, for this is your time, dear one!

All dance or silently still while music is played

two mins or so.
Hold lava piece aloft.

Sister Fire Dancer, fire and healing within are sacred secrets of yours! I wish to learn more so that I may help others! Therefore, with this holy stone, I plead to you and your people that I may share your wisdom and ask for your aid, dear one!

Place the lava piece next to Fire Dancer.
Fire Dancer, We thank you for all aid you have shared. I ask in reverence that I continue to grow in your Sacred Wisdom.

Offering of seeds.
With these seeds, we honor the Sacred sister Fire Dancer. As these seeds grow in fruitfulness, may we grow in your ways.
Continue with Sphere or close in reverse.

DAME RAGNELL
A CLASSIC ARTHURIAN FAERY STORY

On one of his many quests, King Arthur did chance upon a stranger of the Fey, called the Son of Summers day. This man did pose to Arthur a riddle with Arthur's life hung to it and stated that within a period of a twelvemonth, Arthur was to return and answer the riddle or forfeit his life. However, as Arthur was free to go, he noticed a woman dressed in silk out of the mist, but a grotesque appearance showed Arthur's heartfelt pity for her.

This woman, red of face and lumpy with warts, stated her name was Dame Ragnell, and she alone had the answer to the son of summers day's riddle, yet she stated that she would give this answer for a price. That price is that she marries one of the Red Cross Knights. After a long while, Arthur returned to Camelot and told all his tale, and among the laughter amongst his comrades, Gawain met the crone and stated, "I will wed her."

Ignoring the rude comments of his peers, Gawain escorted Dame Ragnell, cackling to herself, to the feasting hall, and as the greedy crone tore at her food, all at the table turned away in disgust. Only Gawain had kind words with his new wife throughout the meal.

Gawain, in his goodwill, led Dame Ragnell, the repulsive crone, past his courtiers and finally into the bridal chamber.

Gawain unbuckled his sword when they were alone, turned, and noticed the old crone was gone. Beside his bed stood a beautiful woman with dark eyes and long, flowing black hair. Gawain dropped his sword and asked, "Who are you?" "Your wife," replied the woman, "I lie under enchantment, and the terms of this enchantment lie with you, Gawain." She replied in a musical tone.

"I can be as you see me when we are alone and a crone when anyone is by, or I can be a crone when we are alone and beautiful in the eyes of others. Choose then, my husband."

Gawain stated, "This is a sad choice, to lose honor for the pleasure of love.' my dear, you must do as you wish. I give a choice to you with all my heart," Dame Ragnell embraced Gawain stating,

"You have answered the terms of the spell that chained me sovereignty of choice is rare and what a woman most desires. You have given me this freedom, I am your true lady, and this is the body I shall always wear."

HANDFASTINGS

A Handfasting is mainly a promise of love stated before the Deities. This ritual must be officiated by someone Ordained to be legal. It is considered a successful fasting if the couple is gifted with a child. There is no grand ritual change rule lest one makes one up. The rituals are always written to meet the couple's needs!

This Hand fasting was written because I needed something explicitly honoring all elements and wholly celebratory. I was significantly In need of a WYRD Draconic Hand fasting that could do this well.

<u>HANDFASTING IN TRADITIONAL CELTIC PAGAN CEREMONIAL FORM</u>

This Rite should be written with the couple's input within these guidelines. Before the ceremony can begin, the area chosen is traditionally swept free of debris and negativity by the Maiden of the Broom. Once done, the ritual commences.

HIGH PRIEST/ESS with the sword, starting at the East, circling deosil, the circle's perimeter three times]: quarter candles are lit. Flower Maiden spreads and decorates with petals

Maiden says;

**Three times around,
Once for the Maiden,
Twice for the MOTHER
Thrice for the CRONE**

Chosen chant or song is sung and or danced to by all.
All within the circle say:

I humbly ask for the attendance of the Elementals of life!

The caller of the East: *(said while igniting incense in censer)* with chosen incense, Holds censer aloft.

Welcome, Powers of Air! With clever fingers, weave the bonds of Heart, Spirit, and Love between these two tightly! Let none undo the fabric of their Love!
(Places censer at the eastern point of circle, bows & retires.)

The caller of the South; *(said while lighting a red candle)*: Hold aloft

Welcome, Powers of Fire! Ignite the Passion and the Love for this blessed pair. Ever burning, yet never consuming one or the other!

(Places candle at the southern point of circle, bows & retires.)

The caller of the West; *[said while pouring saltwater into a bowl]*: hold aloft

Welcome, Powers of Water! Bless this couple with Love as deep as any ocean! May the richness of body, soul, and spirit be theirs evermore!

(Places bowl at the western point of the circle, bows & retires)

The caller of the North: *[said while filling the bowl with soil]*: hold aloft

Welcome, Powers of Earth! Bless this man and woman with thy strength and wisdom to be theirs as long as Love lasts!

(Places bowl at the northern point of circle, bows & retires.)

(Callers of the East, South, West, and North, *(n unison, say)*

Gracious Goddess, Gentle God, Grant this blessed pair thy Love and protection. Blessed Be! Standing before the altar, taking man's right hand and woman's left hand.

We gather here this night/day in a ritual of Love. You two- stand here before your friends, the Elements, the Lord, and Lady, to join together as the beginning of a family. For before there can be three, there must be two.

High Priest/ess *(Joining couple's hands, with them facing each other)*

(---), what do you have to offer this woman for her Love?

Groom *(gets down on one knee)*

Insert grooms, vows

Bride says;

My Love, I accept your pledge!

Priest/ess says:

--- and what do you offer in return for this man's Love?

Bride says vows

Groom says

My Love, I accept your pledge

Hight Priestess *(Binds couple's right hands wrapping with the handfasting ribbon gently)*
May the Lord and Lady smile upon this Union and bless this couple with health and prosperity!

High Priest/ess says:

May neither take advantage of the other. Remember that what one may not provide, the other may!

High Priest/ess sys:

All have now heard your Vows. These gifts, like your vows, are without a beginning or end. Now given, they represent a seal of your Love and respect for each other

High Priest/ess says(Offering food to the couple to eat from.*)*

This is your first food together as a man and wife. May you never hunger.

The couple shares together
High Priest/ess says *(*offering Chalice to the couple to drink from)

This is your first drink together as a man and wife. May you never thirst.

High Priestess *(*positions the besom*)*

This will be your first act of working together as Husband and Wife.

*(*High Pries/ess lead the couple to jump the broom.)

High Priest/ess (Removes binding and holds it overhead)

I present to you Mrs. ---- ---- and her Husband, --- ----.

High Priest/ess says:

We thank the elementals of life for their attendance this day/night and ask them to go forth and herald this union.

The caller of the West (raising bowl overhead)

Hail power of Water! Thank thee for thy attention!
Go forth and announce to all this union!

The caller of the South (raising candle overhead)

Hail power of Fire! Thank thee for thy attention!
Go forth and announce to all this union!

The caller of the East (raising censer overhead)

Hail power of Air! Thank thee for thy attention!
Go forth and announce to all this union!

The caller of the North (raising bowl of the Earth)

Hail powers of the Earth! Thank thee for your attention! Go forth and announce to all this union!

This Handfasting is done in the Old Tradition and New mystical style. The couple wished for a magical Christian/Celtic Pagan ceremony. So I put that together, and so here it is.

High Priest-ess (With sword, starting at the North, circling deosil the parameter of the circle three times)

Three Times Round,
Once for the Maiden
Twice for the mother,

Thrice for the crone

Priest-ess says

Dear loved ones – participants in this fine celebration.
Join us in bringing peace amongst us all.
Please make me a channel of your peace.
Where there is hatred, let me sow your love
Where there is injury, let me bring pardon. Where there is despair, let me bring hope. Where there is darkness, let me bring light. Where there is sadness ever, joy.
O Divine Spirit, grant that I may not so much seek to be consoled as to console.
To be understood as to understand. To be loved as to love with all my heart, mind, body, and soul. For it is in giving to all men that we receive. It is in pardoning that we are pardoned. And in dying that we are born to eternal life!

This wondrous time is when we all celebrate the joyous union of—and his chosen—for they wish us to bear witness to their words and actions on this occasion.

Groom says;

I --- do take thee – to be my wedded wife. To have and to hold, from this day forward, for better or worse, for richer, for poorer, for fairer, or fouler, in sickness and health, to love and cherish with my body and worldly wealth, till death do us part, according to the Divine Holy Sacrament. There unto thee, I pledge my troth.

Bride says;

My love, I accept your pledge!
I – do take thee – to my wedded husband. To have and hold from this day forward, for better or worse, for richer or poorer, in sickness and health. To be bonny and buxom at bed and board, to love and cherish, till death us do part. According to the Divine Holy Sacrament, I pledge my troth there unto thee!

Groom says;

My love, I accept your pledge!

The couple drops hands and prepares the rings to bless;
Priest-ess says;

As a traditional symbol of your union, may your
love burn as strongly as this flame!
Both of them light the Unity Candle in the center of the Altar
All repeat The Great Spirit's words

PRAYER AND BLESSING TO THE GREAT SPIRIT

O GREAT SPIRIT WHO ART IN ALL THINGS
SACRED AND MANY ARE THY NAMES!
THINE REALMS SHALL BE KNOWN!
THINE WILLS SHALL BE DONE!
ON EARTH AS THROUGHOUT THE UNIVERSE!
ALLOW US THE THINGS WE NEED TO LEAD STRONG, LOVING, AND BLISSFUL LIVES!
AS WE SHALL HELP OTHERS TO LEAD STRONG, LOVING, AND BLISSFUL LIVES!
BE PATIENT WITH US AND AID US AS NEEDED
THROUGH OUR TRIALS, FAULTS, AND MISTAKES!
AS WE SHALL BE PATIENT WITH AND AID OTHERS THROUGH THEIR TRIALS, FAULTS, AND MISTAKES!
YOU HAVE MADE IT KNOWN THROUGH YOUR PEOPLE "THAT IN AS MUCH AS YE HAVE DONE FOR LEAST OF THESE, MY CHILDREN, YE HAVE DONE FOR ME!
AND WHAT YE HAVE DONE FOR ME FROM THINE OWN HEART, YE SHALL RECEIVE THREEFOLD UPON THREEFOLD!
LASTLY, GREAT SPIRIT HELP US FOLLOW OUR HEARTS DEEPEST DREAMS THROUGH OUR TRUE, CHOSEN, DESTINED PATHS IN LIFE.
THAT WE SHALL ALWAYS FOLLOW OUR BLISS
EVER AND THUS ANON

SO SHALL IT BE!

Bless these rings, oh Great Spirit! That those who wear and receive them may be ever faithful to another, remain in thy peace, to live and grow old together in love.

Groom says

With this ring, I pledge my body,

(touch the ring to the Brides thumb)

**And my life,
In the name of the Father, Son, and Holy Spirit!**

The Groom slips the ring on the Bride
Bride says

With this ring, I pledge my body

(touch the ring to the groom's thumb)

My honor

Touch ring to the little finger

My life

Touch the ring to the ring finger

In the name of the Father, Son, and Holy Spirit!

Maiden slips the ring on the groom

O eternal Divine Spirit, creator, and preserver of all humankind, giver of all spiritual grace, the author of everlasting life. Send thy blessings on these your children who have been blessed in their name—and – as they live faithfully together so they may perform and keep the vow and covenant they have made. These rings are given and received as a token and pledge. May they hereafter remain in perfect love and peace together, living in thy honorable laws Jesus did enforce.

Priest-ess says

This is your first drink together as a man and wife. May you never thirst in the Divine union of your souls!

Priest-ess binds both hands

As this cord I wind with this cord, I bind. So these two as one, so shall they be!

Lead the couple to besom
This will be your first act of working together as husband and wife. You may kiss once for love, Twice for luck, or thrice for long life! Let what The Divine has joined together, let no man put asunder. I present to you all Sir – and his lady—Couple exits under sword to(to a song of choice.)

SACRED WORDS

I love the Lord s prayer. But I'm afraid I have to disagree with the patriarchal, one-sided, and unbalanced approach it took. I decided to write an altered form and rebalance its Earthly honor/Christian version of many years ago. Many totalitarians in many traditions do not agree, but that is okay; I feel and have been told by many others about the great importance these words have to them, and I'll not deprive others of the same.

PRAYER AND BLESSING TO THE GREAT SPIRIT

O GREAT SPIRIT WHO ART IN ALL THINGS
SACRED AND MANY ARE THY NAMES!
THINE REALMS SHALL BE KNOWN!
THINE WILLS SHALL BE DONE!
ON EARTH AS THROUGHOUT THE UNIVERSE!
ALLOW US THE THINGS WE NEED TO LEAD STRONG, LOVING, AND BLISSFUL LIVES!

AS WE SHALL HELP OTHERS TO LEAD STRONG, LOVING, AND BLISSFUL LIVES!
BE PATIENT WITH US AND AID US AS NEEDED
THROUGH OUR TRIALS, FAULTS, AND MISTAKES!
AS WE SHALL BE PATIENT WITH AND AID OTHERS THROUGH THEIR TRIALS, FAULTS, AND MISTAKES!
YOU HAVE MADE IT KNOWN THROUGH YOUR PEOPLE "THAT IN AS MUCH AS YE HAVE DONE FOR LEAST OF THESE, MY CHILDREN, YE HAVE DONE FOR ME!
AND WHAT YE HAVE DONE FOR ME FROM THINE OWN HEART, YE SHALL RECEIVE THREEFOLD UPON THREEFOLD!
LASTLY, GREAT SPIRIT HELP US FOLLOW OUR HEARTS DEEPEST DREAMS THROUGH OUR TRUE CHOSEN DESTINED PATHS IN LIFE.
THAT WE SHALL ALWAYS FOLLOW OUR BLISS
EVER AND THUS ANON
SO SHALL IT BE!

DRAGON

I AM DRACONIS,
I AM THE DRAGON, SATAN FEAR, THE LIZARD, THE SERPENT, THE FROG, THE DENSE; YOU KNOW ME IN YOUR MODEST DREAMS. I AM THE WHEEL, THE HUB, THE UNFOLDING UNIVERSE. I AM THE BLACK VOID DENSITY IN MANIFESTATION. I AM THE WOMB OF CREATION. I AM WHAT IS YET UNKNOWN, UNCREATED, UNMANIFEST WITHIN YOU.
I AM OLD; YOU HAVE KNOWN ME SINCE TIME BEGAN. I AM THE ORIGINAL THOUGHT, THE ORIGINAL PURPOSE. IT WOULD BE BEST IF YOU WORKED WITH ME AND THROUGH ME. SOME SAY I AM DENSE AND, THEREFORE, UNAPPEALING. YOU MUST OVERCOME DENSITY AS LONG AS YOU ENDURE ON THIS PLANET. HOW ELSE SHALL YOU UNDERSTAND THE NATURE OF SPIRIT AND SPIRITUAL LAW UNLESS YOU CREATE WITHIN THE MATERIAL REALM.
NO PART OF YOUR BODY REMAINS UNTOUCHED BY ME, FOR I AM CREATIVITY, THE ESSENCE OF ALTERABILITY WITHIN YOU
MY MASK IS BLACKNESS, AND MY PURPOSE IS CREATION. I AM THE WOMB, THE MYSTIC POOL. DO NOT SEEK IN TOTAL TO UNDERSTAND ME; MY ESSENCE IS UNFATHOMABLE. I AM THE

DEEPEST YEARNING IN YOUR HEART, THE DEEPEST FEAR IN YOUR MIND. THE ULTIMATE PROCESS OF EXPERIENCE- CREATION USE THE POWER WISELY-I AM DRAGON

PRAYER AND PLAY

I AM CALLING TO THE SPIRITS
I CALL TO THE SPIRIT OF LAUGHING WATER,
I CALL TO THE SPIRIT OF SINGING WIND,
I CALL TO THE SPIRITS OF DANCING FIRE. AND THE SPIRIT OF THE DRUMMING EARTH. SING OF THE MOUNTAIN PRINCE FOR A DAY. I CALL ALL BENEFICIAL DEITIES WITH POSITIVE UNIVERSAL ENERGIES TO AID ME IN ATTRACTING STRENGTH AND LOVE. PEACE, WISDOM, AND UNIVERSAL MAGIC WITHIN THIS SPACE ARE EVER-GROWING! COME WILD ROGUE, FROLICSOME MAID! MERRY WITH MAGIC, REMIND US HOW TO BE CHILDREN WHEN PLAY WAS OUR WORSHIP AND PLEASURE OUR PRAYER! LET US LAUGH OURSELVES SILLY AND THROW OUR CARES TO THE WIND. LET MIRTH BE OUR MAGIC AND HUMOR OUR HYMN.

WE ARE THE FEY

WE ARE FLEET, AND WE ARE FREE
WE ARE ALL THAT WE CAN BE
AIR AND FIR LAND AND SEA
WE ARE THE SACRED; WE ARE THE SIDHE
WE ARE WILD; WE ARE RARE
WE ARE FIERCE, AND WE ARE FAIR
 MORE THAN ANY OTHERS DARE
WE ARE GLORIOUS PAST COMPARE
WE ARE TEMPEST-REARING TALL
WE ARE FOXEN SNEAKING SMALL
WE ARE MUSIC AND ITS CALL
WE ARE DANU'S CHILDREN ALL
WE ARE DUSK, AND WE ARE DAWN
WE ARE SPARKS IMMORTAL SPAWN
THOUGH YOU THINK THAT WE ARE GONE
STILL, WE LAUGH AND LINGER ON
FOR WE CAN NOT FADE AWAY

SO WE GO OUR MERRY WAY
IN THE DUSK OF MORTAL DAY
WE ARE THE FEY!!

WHY

WHY DO YOU HURT ME? DO YOU NOT UNDERSTAND
I LOVE SO DEEPLY. LET ME TAKE YOUR HAND
I SEE YOU WITH THE EYES OF THE OWL
DEEP INTO YOUR SOUL,
MANY SECRETS, FEARS YOU HAVE
YES, DEAR ONE, I KNOW.
YET THESE THINGS I'LL NOT ARTICULATE FOR
SACRED THEY ARE TO YOU
THE OWLS GRACE AND GENTLE MYSTERY IN CARING
I DO WISH TO SHARE WITH YOU
COYOTE HAS TAUGHT ME WELL TO HARNESS THE
BALANCE OF LAUGHTER AND SERIOUSNESS
I PLEAD WITH YOU AS I SEE YOU PRETENDING TO SMILE
AND FALSELY GREET ME. DO SO ONLY IF IT IS IN YOUR HEART
TO BE TRUE!
AS THE OWL, I FEEL YOUR PAIN AND FEAR,
 IF ONLY YOU FELT MINE FOR THE TEARS I SHED FOR THIS
PAIN ARE MANY
AS COYOTE HIDES FROM HIS TORMENTORS WHO FEIGN
UNDERSTANDING
RESPECT FOR HONESTY IS GIVEN BY ALL OF US
I DO NOT UNDERSTAND WHY. WHY DO YOU HURT ME?
I ONLY WISH TO SHARE WITHIN THE SPIRAL THE OLD WITH
THE NEW, AS THE SNAKE-DRAGON SHEDS AND SHARES ITSELF
IN THE NEVER-ENDING SPIRAL.
REMEMBER OF MY PAIN AND THOSE I WILL NOT ARTICULATE,
FOR AS THE SNAKES TONGUE STRIKES AND CAUSES PAIN, SO
I CAN YET WILL NOT
FOR IN MY LOVE OF BALANCE, I WILL HARM NONE IS MY WISH.
 YET TO SHARE THE LOVE AND WISDOM OF COYOTE, OWL, AND
DEAR SNAKE WITH ONLY LOVING TOUCHES.
AS THE OWL VOCALIZES, WHO? ANOTHER IS ASKED IN ITS
SILENT SEARCH FOR ANSWERS TO ITS FLIGHT NEVER-ENDING

WHY?
DO YOU HURT?
KNOW ME FIRST!

I Leave the Charge of the God up to my Priest

CHARGE OF THE GOD

LISTEN TO THE WORDS OF THE GREAT FATHER WHO OF OLD WAS CALLED OSIRIS, ADONIS, ZEUS, THOR, PAN, CERNUNNOS, HERNE, LLUGH, AND BY MANY OTHER NAMES.
MY LAW IS HARMONY WITH ALL THINGS. MINE IS THE SECRET THAT OPENS THE GATE OF LIFE, AND MINE IS THE DISH OF SALT OF THE EARTH. I GIVE THE KNOWLEDGE OF LIFE EVERLASTING, AND BEYOND DEATH, I GIVE THE PROMISE OF REGENERATION AND RENEWAL. I AM THE SACRIFICE, THE FATHER OF ALL THINGS, AND MY PROTECTION BLANKETS THE EARTH. HEAR THE WORDS OF THE DANCING GOD, THE MUSIC OF WHOSE LAUGHTER STIRS THE WINDS, WHOSE VOICE CALLS THE SEASONS. I AM THE LORD OF THE HUNT AND THE POWER OF LIGHT, THE SUN AMONG THE CLOUDS, AND THE SECRET OF THE FLAME! I CALL UPON YOUR BODIES TO ARISE AND COME UNTO ME, FOR I AM THE FLESH OF THE EARTH AND ITS BEINGS. THROUGH ME, ALL THINGS MUST DIE, AND THROUGH ME, ALL THINGS ARE REBORN. LET MY WORSHIP BE IN THE BODY THAT SINGS. FOR BEHOLD, ALL ACTS OF WILLING SACRIFICE ARE MY RITUALS. LET THERE BE DESIRE, FEAR, ANGER, WEAKNESS, JOY, PEACE, AWE, AND LONGING WITHIN YOU, FOR THESE, TOO, ARE PART OF THE MYSTERIES FOUND WITHIN YOURSELF. WITHIN ME, ALL BEGINNINGS HAVE ENDINGS, AND ALL ENDINGS HAVE BEGINNINGS.

CHARGE OF THE DARK GOD
Through Christopher Hutton

LISTEN TO THE WORDS OF THE DARK GOD! WHO WAS OF OLD CALLED DONN ANUBIS, HADES HODER, AND BY MANY OTHER NAMES! I AM THE SHADOW OF THE BRIGHT DAY, AND I AM THE REMINDER OF MORTALITY AT THE HEIGHT OF LIVING! I AM THE

NEVER-ENDING VEIL OF NIGHT WHERE THE GODDESS DANCES; I AM THE DEATH THAT MUST BE SO THAT LIFE MAY CONTINUE! FOR BEHOLD, LIFE IS IMMORTAL BECAUSE THE LIVING MUST DIE. I AM THE POWER THAT SAYS, "NO FURTHER, AND THAT IS ENOUGH" I AM THE THINGS THAT CAN NOT BE SPOKEN OF. I AM THE LAUGHTER AT THE EDGE OF DEATH! SO COME TO ME NOW INTO THE WARM, ENFOLDING DARK.

FEEL MY CARESSES IN THE HANDS, THE MOUTH, AND THE BODY OF THE ONE YOU LOVE, AND BE TRANSFORMED! GATHER IN THE MOONLESS NIGHT. THE DARK MOTHER AND I WILL LISTEN, SING TO US AND CRY OUT! THE POWER WILL BE YOURS TO YIELD! BLOW ME A KISS WHEN THE SKY IS DARK, AND I WILL SMILE, BUT NO KISS RETURNS, FOR MY KISS IS THE FINAL ONE FOR MORTAL FLESH!

MORRIGAN WORDS

I AM THE ETERNAL MORRIGHAN. I AM THE FIRE OF FIRES
I AM THE FURY THAT DRIVES ALL WARS; I AM THE LUST THAT BURNS MEN'S SOULS. I AM THE DARK SIGIL OF THE UNDER REALM.
I AM THE NIGHTMARE THAT HAUNTS ALL MEN. I AM THE DREAM THAT FEEDS ON DEATH. I AM THE BEAN SIDE KEEN OF THE RAVEN. COME TO ME WHEN YOU FEEL RAGE. COME TO ME IF YOU'VE BEEN SCORNED. I WILL BE THEIR VENGEANCE. I WILL BE THEIR PAIN!

CHARGE OF THE GODDESS HECATE

THE ANCIENT PRIMAL SEASON OF THE WITCH IS HERE. I FORCE YOU TO LAUGH AT YOUR DEATH. But, IF YOU WISH TO HONOR ME, I WILL TAKE YOUR FEARS OF DEATH AWAY AND MAKE YOU GLAD. I AM THE KEEPER OF THE ALTARS, OUTDOORS AND INSIDE. I AM SPEAKING THROUGH YOU WHEN YOU FEEL THE DESIRE TO STAND ALONE AND TALK TO THE FULL MOON. I AM THE WID PART OF YOU, YOUR SIXTH SENSE. THE ONE THAT GIVES YOU HUNCHES, PREMONITIONS, AND DREAMS. I AM THE PRIESTESS IMMORTALALL HALLOWS IS HERE; SOULS COME TO

VISIT, AND THE LIVING WORLD THROWS A PARTY TO MINGLE WITH THE DEAD. I SHARE IN YOUR MERRIMENT!

<u>A FRIEND</u>

IF I COULD CATCH A RAINBOW, I'D DO IT JUST FOR YOU AND SHARE WITH YOU ITS BEAUTY ON THE DAYS YOU'RE FEELING BLUE.
IF I COULD CATCH A MOUNTAIN YOU COULD CALL YOUR VERY OWN, A PLACE TO FIND SERENITY, A PLACE TO BE ALONE AND TAKE YOUR TROUBLES, ID TOSS THEM IN THE SEA! BUT ALL OF THESE THINGS I'M FINDING ARE IMPOSSIBLE FOR ME. I CAN NOT BUILD A MOUNTAIN OR CATCH A RAINBOW FAIR, BUT LET ME BE WHAT I KNOW BEST A FRIEND WHO IS ALWAYS THERE.

<u>WALK WITH ME</u>
<u>(WORDS FROM THE DIVINE TO ALL)</u> I LIKE TO BELIEVE

WHY DO YOU WALK WITH TIMID STEPS AND BOWED HEADS? YOU ARE NOT A SERVANT. FEAR DO NOT SHOW. LET US SHOW YOU THE WAY TO LIGHT THE PATH ON YOUR OWN!

WALK TALL WITH ME SO THAT I MAY HOLD YOU. I AM THE MOTHER, THE EARTH, THE ALL. YOU ARE MY CHILD, MINE TO PROTECT, WALK WITH ME.

WALK STRONG WITH ME SO THAT I MAY TEACH YOU. I AM THE FATHER OF THE LIGHT. THE SUN, YOU ARE MY STUDENT, MY LIGHT YOU SHALL SEE, WALK WITH ME.
WALK QUIETLY WITH ME SO THAT I MAY INSPIRE YOU. I AM THE YOUTH, THE WILL. YOU ARE MY FRIEND. TOGETHER WE ARE STRONG. WALK WITH ME.

WALK QUIETLY WITH ME SO THAT I MAY INFUSE YOU. I AM THE BEAUTY, THE LOVE, THE FLOWER. YOU ARE MY FRIEND; WE EMBODY LOVE AND WALK WITH ME.

WALK FAST WITH ME SO THAT I MAY STRENGTHEN YOU. I AM THE FORGE, THE CRAFT, THE STRENGTH. YOU ARE MY PROJECT. MY CRAFT FLOWS THROUGH YOU WALK WITH ME.

WALK SILENTLY WITH ME SO THAT I MAY SHOW YOU. I AM THE DARK, THE PAST, THE SHADOW. YOU ARE MY COMPANION. I HAVE THE PAST YOU SEEK. WALK WITH ME.

WALK THE SKY WITH ME, THAT I MAY RAISE YU. I AM THE MOON, THE STARS, AND THE NIGHT. YOU ARE MY SHADOW. MY CAULDRON INSPIRES. WALK WITH.

WALK NATURE WITH ME THAT I MAY SHOW YOU. I AM THE FOREST, THE ANIMALS, THE LAND. YOU ARE MY PARTNER, MY CHAMPION ON EARTH. WALK WITH ME.

INCENSES AND USES

I use these regularly for effectiveness.
Choose any three of these to make your own. For each recipe

Sacred space Incense

Brass filings, 1/8 tsp Cedar, 1/8 tsp Sage, ¼ tsp Frankincense powder, ¼ tsp Myrrh powder, 1/8 tsp Dragons Blood powder, 1/8 tsp Passion Flower, 1/8 tsp Lavender, 1/16 tsp dried apple, ¼ tsp Patchouli, ¼ tsp Willow, seven drops any flower essential oil. Grind in a coffee grinder, and it is ready!

Draconis Incense

One ¼ Dragons blood, one ¼ Myrrh or Lily powder, 3/4 tsp Yellow Dock or Bistort, ¾ Patchouli or Amber PWD/ or Amber oil ten drops. Any amt. of Snakeskin or Lizard skin.
Continually charge with Lodestone.

Invoking Incense

Brass filings, 1/2 tsp Cinamon PWD. ¼ tsp. Calendula Flowers, 21 drops of Cinnamon oil, 21 drops, Frankincense oil, ½ tsp. ¼ tsp. Yellow Dock owd. Frankincense powder 1/4 tsp. Turmeric od sage.,1/6 rue/1/6 Rosemary or Pepper. 1/8 tsp Rose, ¼ tsp lavender, ¼ tsp Copal, ½ tsp Passion Flower. Add any amt of a coyote or rabbit fur.
Grind

Banishing Incense

Iron filings1/16 tsp, 1/8 Dragons blood, ¼ Myrrh, 1/8 Tobasco chili peppers or Cayenne pepper. ¼ tsp Rue, Any drops of patchouly.
Grind

Samhain Incense

Remember, you can use any three of these herbs.

1/8 tsp. Nettle, 1/8 tsp. Bay leaf, 1/8 tsp. Sage, 1/8 tsp Tarragon or Basil. ¼ tsp. Calendula, six Oak leaves, Seven drops, Frankincense and Myrrh oil, 1/8 tsp. lavender, 1/8 tsp Sandalwood, 1/8 tsp. Dittany of Crete, 1/8 tsp.Dragons Blood.
Grind

Yule Incense

1/8 tsp, pine needles, 1/8 tsp cinnamon, 1/8 tsp. Frankincense, 1/8 ts. Holly. 1/8 tsp apple, six oak leaves.
Grind

Imbolc Incense

¼ tsp. Heather, ¼ tsp, Tulip, ¼ Sage, ¼ tsp Chamomile, ¼ tsp. Passion Flower, 1/8 tsp Dragon Blood.
Grind

Ostara incense

¼ tsp Patchouly, Tulip flowers, ¼ tsp, Lavendar, ¼ tsp Vervain, 1 tsp Frankincense, 1 tsp Benzoin, 1 Tsp Pine resin bark, bunny hair. Grind

Beltane Incense

1/8 tsp. Marjoram, 1/8 tsp. Nettle, 1/8 tsp Broom, 1/8 tsp. Woodruff, 2 drops Honeysuckle oil, 1/8 tsp. Dragons Blood, 1/8 tsp, Frankinsence, 1/8 tsp. Copal.
Grind

Lughnasadh Incense

Equal parts of any three ingredients.

Dried Rose Petals, Dried Apple, Moss, Wheat, Basil, Dragons blood, Cedar, three drops of fir oil, and three drops of almond oil. Charge with a crystal and a garnet.

Mabon Incense

CITATIONS

Recommended Reading These are guidelines, books, and movies that have inspired me. I have used these to enhance Draconis myself; even though I know people's different needs, I still want to share them with others.

Websites

(2022, December 12). ArcticServer/NorthPoleServer – Forged from Alaska Spirit!. https://northpoleserver.com
(n.d.). Faerie Faith. https://faeriefaith.net
(n.d.). Grove of Nova Scotia Druids. https://www.druidry.ca

(1996). *Dragonheart* [Film].

References

Hubble Space Telescope images. NASA NASA.gov
(n.d.). STRENGTH. Boy scout trail. https://www.boyscouttrail.com/skits.asp

(n.d.). CATCH A RAINBOW. SCRAPBOOK. heartswithsoul.com/ catch_rainbow.htm
(n.d.). CHARGE OF THE DARK GOD. SPELLS OF MAGIC. https:// www.spellsofmagic.com/coven_ritual.html?ritual=1522&coven=6
https://www.scotclans.com/pages/robert-the-bruce-and-the-spider
(n.d.). FISHERMAN'S WIFE. WIKIPEDIA. https://en.wikipedia.org/ wiki/The_Fisherman_and_His_Wife
https://storiestogrowby.org/story/sir-gawain-the-lady-ragnell/
(2003). ANIMAL SPEAK/ Ted Andrews. Winston Allen
(1582701709). THE SECRET/Rhonda Byrne. Atria Books.
DANCING WITH DRAGONS. 1567181651, 1998.
HAWKING, S. (1988). A BRIEF HISTORY OF TIME. BANTAM BOOKS
Kondratiev, A. (1998). The Apple Branch. Kensington.
Campbell, J., & Moyers, B. D. (1988). The power of myth.
Konstantinos. (2002). Nocturnal witchcraft: Magick after dark. Llewellyn Worldwide.
Konstantinos. (2002). Gothic grimoire. Llewellyn Worldwide.
Pagels, E. (1989). The Gnostic Gospels. Vintage.
Skinner, S. (2007). *The Complete Magician's tables: The most complete set of magic, Kabbalistic, angelic, astrologic, alchemic, demonic, geomantic, grimoire, gematria, I ching, tarot, planetary, Pagan Pantheon, plant, perfume, emblem and character correspondences in more than 777 tables.* Llewellyn Worldwide.
In *the power of myth.* (n.d.).
Walker, B. G. (1996). *Women's encyclopedia of myths and secrets.* Book Sales.
Walker, B. G. (2013). *The woman's dictionary of symbols and sacred objects.* HarperCollins.

The SACRED SPIRAL interprets many mystical philosophies and rites regarding how they correspond to many facets of our everyday human life. Quantum physics is used to aid in understanding these techniques and interpreting for us how these fundamental theories impact our daily lives.

www.ingramcontent.com/pod-product-compliance
Lightning Source LLC
LaVergne TN
LVHW041840070526
838199LV00045BA/1365